SEX & MORALS

IDEAS IN ACTION

GENERAL EDITOR: Maurice Cranston

SEX & MORALS

C.H. and Winifred M.Whiteley

CULTURE &
DISCOVERY

BASIC BOOKS, Inc., Publishers
New York

Contents

SEX & MORALS

I

Why is there Sexual Morality?

How difficult it is to be reasonable about sex! The trouble is that it is such an emotionally disturbing topic. We cannot think about it without some activation of our sexual impulses . . . unless of course we are past the time of life for it and no longer want to consider it anyway. The organic disturbance is further reinforced by taboos and inhibitions built up through our sex education. Whatever the society we have been brought up in, there are some types of sexual behaviour we have been trained to react to as disgusting or unnatural. These vary from one social group to another, but few people realise how much they can vary even between different classes in the same country. So sex is a ticklish subject, which we all approach alerted for shocks and disagreements. If we have to discuss it face to face there may be embarrassment; there are prudent silences when we keep our reflections to ourselves, or unexpected explosions of indignation, even between old acquaintances. Anyone who says bluntly what he thinks about a sexual problem in English-speaking countries can be certain of angering some people, very likely among his personal friends. In expressing our own opinions in this book, we, the authors, have done our best to be reasonable in spite of the conditioning we have received, and we hope that our readers are prepared to do the same.

There is another reason why it is hard to think rationally about sexual matters, which is that the value and purpose of rules of sexual morality are not always obvious. At first sight the rules, unlike those against violence and theft, seem arbitrary and superfluous. But we should first seek the justification for them. Usually there is some justification and it is we who are being irrational if we do not try to find it. The purpose of this book is to examine the principal types of sex morality, to ask what is the purpose, and what are the advantages and disadvantages of each, and ultimately to reach some tentative conclusions about the sort of sex morality most suitable to our own society. The conclusions can only be tentative, because it is so hard to tell just what effects different sexual customs have on the lives and happiness of people who adopt them.

Where we do not know the effects on human well-being of a given pattern of sexual behaviour, emotion and superstition tend to take over. Because sexual impulses are very strong, especially in young people, strong feelings have to be evoked to restrain them—strong convictions that this is right, that is wrong. Sexual education aims at arousing and reinforcing such convictions, and once these are active in us, we do not stop to consider what good or ill effects various sexual practices actually produce: we only look for arguments to justify our convictions. We do not want to understand. Consequently the arguments advanced in favour of particular opinions concerning sex morality are often bad ones. There is no topic more burdened with false statements and weak arguments.*

Here are a few of the old wives' tales about sexual matters which are or have been believed by various human communities:

That a woman can be made pregnant by kissing or heavy petting, without intercourse.
That children conceived during menstruation are born deformed.
That a woman's thoughts during pregnancy influence the character of her child.
That if a woman has twins, the father of one of them is a devil.
That you can tell the size of a man's penis by the length of his nose.
That if a man is touched by menstrual blood he will fall ill.
That one contraceptive in every batch is a dud.
That the children of incestuous unions are monsters.
That masturbation can drive one insane.

* See R. Atkinson, *Sexual Morality*, for a criticism of the arguments.

That if a girl does not bleed when she is penetrated, she is not a virgin.

That it is dangerous to wash one's hair when menstruating.

That hair on the chest is a sign of manliness.

That venereal disease can be contracted by having intercourse during menstruation.

That homosexuality is incurable.

That all homosexuals have womanish tastes.

That if a man commits adultery during his wife's pregnancy the baby will die.

That hard exercise lessens sexual desire.

That foreigners are more lascivious than natives. (This is current in all countries.)

That women of primitive races suffer less in childbirth than civilised women.

That all women are fond of children.

Some of these opinions are held in primitive societies; some, no less absurd, in our own. All of them are quite false. One of the silliest, that relating to the effects of masturbation, was widely held by doctors and expounded in medical textbooks, though there was never any evidence for its truth and a serious investigation would easily have disproved it. This shows that even thoughtful professional men can base their beliefs about sex on their emotions instead of on evidence. It is obvious that such a belief has its origin in the desire to find some telling argument that will persuade people not to masturbate. So we find that opinions about sexual right and wrong are commonly supported, not by reference to actual effects, but by 'myths'—that is, groups of tales and assertions, partly true and partly false, accepted and propagated not because of what truth they do have, but because they support and justify a set of moral rules.

The difficulty of basing sexual morality on *true* opinions has been increased because persons in authority have often tried hard to prevent the truth from being discovered and stated. They have believed that the best way to keep people (especially young people) obedient to the rules is to keep them ignorant of the relevant facts, that in this field of human behaviour knowledge is corrupting. Sometimes the myths and superstitions have actually been spread by influential people. Sometimes the authorities have achieved the same purpose by preventing open mention of the facts about reproduction (some Victorian textbooks of anatomy omitted the sexual organs), about contraception, venereal disease or prostitution, so that people were left at the mercy of whatever tall stories they happened to encounter. It is still the custom in many families for children to be given no information about how babies are produced and about the function of their own sexual parts; and the information they do get is picked up in garbled and fantastic forms from other children.

A wise morality, in sex as in all other matters, cannot be based on ignorance. An enlightened society will do its utmost to discover and adopt those rules which benefit human happiness and liberate human talents. We do not underestimate the difficulty of finding out which rules these are. But that is no excuse for not trying.

The first thing to do is examine the records of human societies and see how many different kinds of sexual morality have been tried and found possible. If there are rules that no human society has been able to dispense with, it is unlikely that our own society can dispense with them. But if we find a rule which some societies insist on while others do not bother, we may ask whether that rule serves any useful purpose. In what respects do human societies agree and in what do they differ, about sexual right and wrong?

If with this question in mind we survey what has been written about the sexual customs of the human race, savage and civilised, our first impression is of an enormous diversity. In some societies, like our own, a man may have only one wife at a time and a woman only one husband. But societies which allow some sort of polygamy are far more common. Usually it is the man who is allowed several wives—in Mohammedan countries up to four, in some others as many as he can afford. But there are also a few communities in which a woman can have more than one husband. Sometimes the joint wives of one man have to be sisters, or the joint husbands of one woman brothers; sometimes this is not required, or it may even be forbidden.

Once a couple are married, divorce may be impossible; or it may be granted by a tribunal if one of the parties can show valid grounds;

or it may be possible for husband or wife to dissolve the marriage simply by leaving or dismissing the other partner. Sometimes either party can divorce the other, sometimes only the husband has this right. Adultery, infertility, desertion, cruelty, insanity, laziness, are valid grounds for divorce among some peoples, but not among others. In some societies a married couple are forbidden to have intercourse except with each other. But there are a large number in which some kinds of extramarital sex are regarded as blameless. A man may be allowed intercourse with his wife's sister, or with his own cousin, or with slave women or prostitutes, without breaking any moral rule. Some people offer their wives to guests for the night, and some practise the temporary borrowing or exchanging of wives, especially where men are long away from home. Others have periodical festivals at which all the usual sexual prohibitions are in abeyance. On the other hand, a man may not be allowed to mate with his own wife whenever he wishes: intercourse may be forbidden during menstruation, in the later stages of pregnancy, while she is suckling a child, or on some important occasion such as a harvest, a religious ceremony or a military expedition.

There are societies in which young people are expected to be chaste until they are married; others which apply this rule to girls only; others which take no notice of premarital sex unless it leads to the birth of children; and others again which do not mind even this, and allow the unmarried complete sexual liberty.

In some parts of the world a marriage requires the consent of the bride and the groom but of nobody else, and only their free choice can bring it about. In others, a girl may be given in marriage to whomever her parents choose, without regard for her wishes; and sometimes this applies to boys as well, who may be married or betrothed in infancy. (In human history as a whole, arranged marriages have probably been far more numerous than free ones.) Girls of some tribes cannot be married unless their bridegrooms pay a bride price to their parents for them; girls of other tribes cannot be married unless their fathers provide them with dowries. (Both these customs serve a similar purpose: they enhance the girl's value and they act as a check against divorce, since if there is a divorce the bride price or dowry must usually be returned.)

Plainly there is no 'normal' or 'natural' pattern of sex morality. Customs differ widely, and primitive peoples differ more among themselves than civilised ones. So there is no question of attributing human sexual morality to instinctive repugnances arising in the course of nature. The repugnances that we have are divergent and learned, the outcome of training which in itself is traditional. If they were inborn they would display more or less the same pattern in all peoples, which they do not. The same objection applies to the notion of a natural moral law which any thoughtful person can discover for himself. Amazonian Indians, Polynesians and modern Japanese, like the ancient Greeks, feel no shame at being seen naked; other peoples regard bare knees, bare cheeks, bare noses or bare genitals as indecent. Neither instinct nor natural law can explain reticences so diverse. Nor will they explain why the young men of some tribes refuse to marry a girl who is a virgin, while the young men of other tribes will not marry one who is not. Our ideas of sexual right and wrong are customary and we learn them from other people; it follows that they can be changed. Such changes, involving the learning of new customs, new shames and revulsions, have happened many times in history. Sometimes they have been brought about by conquerors imposing their ideas on their subjects, sometimes through the influence of religious doctrine, sometimes by pressure from interested groups. We ourselves appear to be in process of changing our ideas of sexual morality; and we are in a better position than our ancestors, because of our greater knowledge of human nature and history, to consider what changes it would be wise to make.

How do any sexual customs become established?

In man the sexual impulse is both powerful and persistent; the human race is always sexually 'in season'. Having to restrain our sexual impulses is therefore highly disagreeable. If men have everywhere imposed restrictions on sexual behaviour, they must have been impelled by strong incentives. Now there is no record of a society in which anything approaching general promiscuity is allowed. All human groups distinguish between sex that is permitted and sex that is not. For most, the permitted sex relations form only a small part of the physically possible ones. The situation is parallel to those regarding the aggressive and acquisitive urges. Obviously if human beings are to dwell together in a society, co-operating comfortably to make a living, they must restrain their urges to fight one another and grab whatever comes to hand. Without customary restraints there would be so much violence and insecurity that life would be unbearable. So it is necessary to train children from infancy to control their aggressiveness and respect the property of others. These lessons are hard to learn, since they involve modification of a great deal of spontaneous impulse. The state of primitive communism, in which everyone had the right to take what he needed, is as purely imaginary as the state of natural promiscuity in which every man could sleep with any woman he fancied. But while it is a necessity of survival (and in that sense a 'law of nature') that these impulses should be restrained, there is a wide range of possible methods of restraint and of particular rules distinguishing right aggression from wrong, right appropriation from wrong. What shall count as permissible violence, whether one may beat one's wife, children or servants, kill the thief, the adulterer or the stranger, fight duels, or kick the opposing scrum-half, are matters of convention. Rules of property are even more variable. So it is with the sexual instinct too. Some measure of restraint on it has been found necessary in all human communities, but the details of this restraint are a matter of convention. We must therefore try to account for codes of sexual morality in terms of the necessities and conveniences of human life, and in those same terms we shall try to assess proposals for amending our own conventions.

Amongst the diversities of customs we come upon two important respects in which there is universal agreement. One of these is the rule against incest. Every society prohibits any form of sexual relationship between close relatives, and this may be taken as a first principle of sex morality. But societies are by no means agreed on who is to count as a close relative. The members of the nuclear family—father and mother, sons and daughters, sisters and brothers, grandparents and grandchildren—are always included. But some codes prohibit intercourse between first cousins, others between second, third or fourth cousins. Some count relationships with in-laws as incestuous. Some distinguish between the mother's and the father's relatives, and permit a man to marry his father's sister's daughter but not his mother's sister's daughter, or the other way round. And some, notably in Australia, extend the prohibited degrees of relationship so widely that most of the women a man meets are forbidden to him on grounds of blood relationship. However incest is defined, it is everywhere regarded with a peculiar horror, differing in intensity from the emotion aroused by other breaches of the sex code. The strength of this feeling makes plausible the view that we have an instinctive aversion from incest. But this hardly explains the facts. Men sometimes are sexually attracted by their mothers, sisters or daughters, and from time to time cases of incest do occur, though these are not often reported in the newspapers. Indeed, incest was systematically practised by the Egyptian and Peruvian royal families in order to ensure that both king and queen were of royal blood. In none of these people is anti-incest instinct at work. Nor would instinct explain why in some peoples revulsion is felt against inter-course with aunts, nieces and cousins, with certain classes of in-laws, or with an entire segment of the tribe, or why in some tribes mothers' relatives are banned as mates but not fathers', or vice versa, while in others, including our own, the prohibition is limited to relatives in the direct line.

The explanation of the incest ban has nothing to do with the dis-advantages of in-breeding either, for these, such as they are, were unknown to primitive societies. It is quite a simple one. A family circle within which there is sexual attraction and therefore sexual competition, such as father and son competing for the favours of daughter or mother, would be subject to intolerable strains. A father who is his daughter's lover cannot effectively fulfil his fatherly role towards her; at the same time he is blocking her opportunities of herself becoming a wife and mother in another family circle. Mother and daughter competing for the father's attention would be per-petually at strife. Other men and women looking for mates would first have to seduce the children from the sexual attentions of their parents. Clearly this is no valid way of conducting family life. Parents should be providers, guides, teachers and wielders of authority, ready to initiate their children into the wider society; sexual interest in them would interfere with these tasks. There are similar reasons for prohibiting sexual relationships between brothers and sisters. A taboo on incest is necessary to human society if there is to be family life at all. Extensions of the taboo beyond the nuclear family come either from applying the rules without thought for their purpose, or from the need to keep growing teenagers from brawling with those groups they will most often meet within the extended family.

The institution of marriage is the other feature common to all societies in their organisation of sex life. By marriage we mean the fairly permanent sexual, social and economic co-operation of a man with a woman, normally preceded by some civil or religious ceremony. The ceremony is the usual prelude to marital co-operation; it gives formal notice of the couple's new status and intentions, and invests them with rights and duties enforceable at law. In the view of many religious people, a genuine marriage can be brought into existence only by a religious ceremony: the couple make their solemn vows in the sight of God, and He creates a unique 'metaphysical' bond between them; all couples not so united are living 'in sin'. We personally do not find this 'metaphysical' idea of marriage intelligible and it seems to us that the essential purposes of marriage may sometimes be fulfilled by a couple who have not gone through any official ceremony, and may fail to be fulfilled by a couple who have done so. Many atheists and nonconformists have refused to be officially married because the only legal ceremony was one belonging to a religious faith which they did not share. Others refuse as a gesture of defiance to society at large. Such people may intend and achieve a faithful and affectionate union. Nevertheless, a man who lives with a woman without marrying her deprives her of the legal safeguards against his deserting or failing to maintain her, and his children of the legal advantages of legitimacy, whatever they may be. He must always come under the suspicion that his motive for evading the ceremony is to remain free to abandon his responsibilities. Why is marriage necessary? It serves two obvious purposes, and so long as these purposes remain to be served, there will be marriage. Firstly it provides a home for the children. Normally the mother who bore the child both wants and is obliged by custom to look after it. But biological paternity creates no such close tie between father and child, and in many animal species paternity is unrecognised. Having begotten a child nine months previously, often unintentionally, a man is not automatically predisposed to take any interest in it when it is born. He wants persuading. But the child needs both parents. He needs his father's earnings to support him while his mother is busy looking after him. Later he will need fatherly training, and if he is a boy, the model of manliness that a father provides. One of the few facts about the development of human personality of which psychologists are confident is that in any culture a child with both parents in his home is better off than a child with only one. Thus marriage grows out of the needs of the family, and not the family out of marriage. Marriage is required as a device for nurturing children, work that few mothers can successfully undertake single-handed. No other animal needs parents for a dozen or more years, and no other animal has them. So the abolition of family life is only conceivable in a society which makes communal provision for bringing up its children. It is significant that no society has in fact found an alternative way, and that the alternatives tried out in our own society for the upbringing of children whose parents are dead, absent or inadequate, have been generally judged inferior in efficacy even to poor-quality parents. The primary function of the family then is to tie the father to the mother and children so long as they cannot fend for themselves. Marriage secures to him the mother's services as sexual partner, worker and companion, while it assures her of his financial and moral support. To some men children are part of the price to be paid for having a woman of their own. But a sensible society will see to it that the children themselves represent a gain. They can become economically useful through work in the family farm or business. They may be customarily or legally required to take over their father's responsibilities as he grows older and to care for him in the later years of his life. Children's support of their parents is as important a part of the family system as the parents' support of their children; it enables human life to be prolonged beyond the stage where an individual can support himself. So building up a family of one's own as a source of wealth, and perhaps even more of personal prestige, becomes a dominant human interest. These functions have only slight relation to biological paternity. Indeed there exist societies in which a man takes responsibility for his wife's children without asking whether they are his offspring or not, and may even feel flattered if some outstanding person will father a child for him to rear. There are other societies where his responsibility is for his sister's children and not for those of his wife.

Marriage fulfils another important need often overlooked by its critics: it shares out sexual opportunity in a fairly even way so that everyone gets one share and knows his or her rights and duties. A society without marriage, the promiscuous society which some naïve theorists have imagined, would be one of incessant competition, intrigue, jealousy and violence, in which a man never knew where his next sex experience was coming from. To get a partner he would have every time to persuade, pay or coerce a woman. There would be fierce rivalry for the attractive mates and nothing for the rest, and a vast amount of energy would be squandered in sexual competition. This way of life is sometimes found among people who have few other responsibilities, but obviously it would be too disruptive for the majority with their living to earn and children to rear.*

So far we have dealt only with the man's side of the picture. Of late there have been women too who wanted to call themselves 'free' and raise children on their own, whether as widows, divorcees or unmarried persons.† But the strain of being at once breadwinner, home-maker and mentor to children can scarcely be appreciated by those who have never undertaken it. One individual cannot really do the work of two. If in addition the 'free woman' feels, as most women do, the need to be loved by a man with affection as well as sexual desire, her position cannot be anything but painful. Few men give of their best to a woman to whom they are not tied. It is the tie that brings into being the loyalty between husband and wife. Women need emotional security more than men do; at bottom few of them want to be 'free'—they want a reliable partner who will share their responsibilities.

So marriage has the multiple role of providing a satisfactory upbringing for children, stable sexual partnership and the expectation of support in their old age for the parents, and emotional security and companionship for all. The entire system of sexual morality can be understood as a means of maintaining family life so that all may profit.

* The fundamental nastiness of promiscuous living is well shown in Henry Miller's *Tropic of Cancer*.
† See, for instance, Doris Lessing's *Golden Notebook*.

2

The Patriarchal Attitude

and the Myth of Womanliness

In this chapter we shall examine a particular view of sexual morality which we shall call the patriarchal view. Moralities of a patriarchal type have been found in many different communities, with differences in detail but an underlying similarity of attitude. We shall take as a specimen the sexual morality of the ancient Hebrews, as it is expressed in the rules of the Old Testament. These are the essential rules:

> If a man commits adultery with the wife of his neighbour, both the adulterer and the adulteress shall be put to death. The man who lies with his father's wife has uncovered his father's nakedness; both of them shall be put to death. . . . If a man lies with his daughter-in-law, both of them shall be put to death; they have committed incest. . . . If a man lies with a male as with a woman, both of them have committed an abomination; they shall be put to death. If a man takes a wife and her mother also, it is wickedness; they shall be burned with fire, both he and they. If a man lies with a beast, he shall be put to death; and you shall kill the beast. If a woman approaches any beast and lies with it, you shall kill the woman and the beast. If a man takes his sister . . . and sees her nakedness and she sees his nakedness, it is a shameful thing, and they shall be cut off in the sight of the children of their people. If a man lies with a woman having her sickness, and uncovers her nakedness he has made naked her fountain, and she has uncovered

the fountain of her blood; both of them shall be cut off from among their people. You shall not uncover the nakedness of your mother's sister or of your father's sister, for that is to make naked one's near kin; they shall bear their iniquity. If a man lies with his uncle's wife, he has uncovered his uncle's nakedness; they shall bear their sin, they shall die childless. If a man takes his brother's wife, it is impurity; he has uncovered his brother's nakedness; they shall be childless [*Leviticus*, XX, 10–21].

You shall not take a woman as a rival wife to her sister, uncovering her nakedness while her sister is yet alive [*Leviticus*, XVIII, 18].

If any man takes a wife and goes into her, and then spurns her and charges her with shameful conduct, and brings an evil name upon her, saying 'I took this woman, and when I came near her I did not find in her the tokens of virginity', then the father of the young woman and her mother shall take and bring out the tokens of her virginity to the elders of the city in the gate; and the father of the young woman shall say to the elders, 'I gave my daughter to this man to wife, and he spurns her; and lo, he has made shameful charges against her, saying "I did not find in your daughter the tokens of virginity". And yet these are the tokens of my daughter's virginity.' And they shall spread the garment before the elders of the city. Then the elders of the city shall take that man and whip him; and they shall fine him 100 shekels of silver, and give them to the father of the young woman, because he has brought an evil name upon a daughter of Israel; and she shall be his wife; he may not put her away all his days. But if the thing is true, that the tokens of virginity were not found in the young woman, then they shall bring out the young woman to the door of her father's house, and the men of her city shall stone her to death with stones, because she has wrought folly in Israel by playing the harlot in her father's house.

If a man is found lying with the wife of another man, both of them shall die, the man who lay with the woman and the woman. If there is a betrothed virgin, and a man meets her in the city and lies with her, then you shall bring them both out to the gate of that city, and you shall stone them to death with stones, the young woman because she did not cry for help though she was in the city, and the man because he violated his neighbour's wife. But if in the open country a man meets a young woman who is betrothed, and the man seizes her and lies with her, then only the man who lay with her shall die. But to the young woman you shall do nothing ... because ... though the betrothed young woman cried for help there was no one to rescue her. If a man meets a virgin who is not betrothed, and seizes her and lies with her, and they are found, then the man who lay with her, shall give to the father of the young woman 50 shekels of silver, and she shall be his wife, because he has violated her; he may not put her away all his days [*Deuteronomy*, XXII, 13–29].

If a man lies carnally with a woman who is a slave, betrothed to another man and not yet ransomed or given her freedom, an inquiry shall be held. They shall not be put to death, because she was not free; but he shall bring a guilt offering for himself to the Lord ... and the sin which he has committed shall be forgiven him [*Leviticus*, XIX, 20–22].

When a man takes a wife and marries her, if then she finds no favour in his eyes because he has found some indecency in her, and he writes her a bill of divorce and puts it in her hand and sends her out of his house, and she departs out of his house, and if she goes and becomes another man's wife, and the latter husband dislikes her and writes her a bill of divorce and puts it in her hand and sends her out of his house, or if the latter husband dies who took her to be his wife, then her former husband who sent her away may not take her again to be his wife, after she has been defiled; for that is an abomination before the Lord [*Deuteronomy*, XXIV, 1–4].

If brothers dwell together, and one of them dies and has no son, the wife of the dead shall not be married outside to a stranger; her husband's brother shall go into her, and take her as his wife. ... And the first son whom she bears shall succeed to the name of his brother who is dead, that his name may not be blotted out of Israel [*Deuteronomy*, XXV, 5–9].

He whose testicles are crushed or whose male member is cut off shall not enter the assembly of the Lord. No bastard shall enter the assembly of the Lord; even to the tenth generation none of his descendants shall enter the assembly of the Lord [*Deuteronomy*, XXIII, 1–2].

There shall be no cult prostitute of the daughters of Israel, neither shall there be a cult prostitute of the sons of Israel [*Deuteronomy*, XXIII, 17].

When a man sells his daughter as a slave, she shall not go out as the male slaves do. If she does not please her master, who has designed her for himself, then he shall let her be redeemed, since he has dealt faithlessly with her [*Exodus*, XXI, 7–8].

When you go forth to war against your enemies, and the Lord God gives them into your hands, and you take them captive, and see among the captives a beautiful woman, and you have desire for her and would take her for yourself as a wife, then you shall bring her home to your house . . . and she shall remain in your house and bewail her father and her mother a full month; after that you may go into her and be her husband, and she shall be your wife. Then, if you have no delight in her, you shall let her go where she will, but you shall not sell her for money, since you have humiliated her [*Deuteronomy*, XXI, 10–14].

A woman shall not wear anything that pertains to a man, nor shall a man put on a woman's garment; for whoever does these things is an abomination to the Lord your God [*Deuteronomy*, XXII, 5].

This code of rules has three striking features.

Firstly, it is a strict morality. The condemnation of adultery, incest, premarital unchastity, homosexuality and bestiality is unconditional, and the commonest penalty is death.

Secondly, it is a morality with a double standard. The rules imposed on women are much more severe than those imposed on men. A bride must be a virgin on her wedding day, or she may be stoned to death; but there is no similar requirement for the bridegroom. A woman offends against the law if she mates with anyone except her husband. But a man is not similarly restricted to one woman. He does indeed suffer the same penalty as the woman if he seduces the wife or fiancée of his neighbour. But he may take several wives (the leading figures of the Old Testament usually did so). He may buy female slaves and use them as his concubines (a wife would sometimes give her husband one of her own slaves for this purpose, as both of Jacob's wives did). And nothing is said against his making use of prostitutes. Again, divorce is entirely at the will of the husband. He may expel his wife if he is dissatisfied with her for any reason at all; his word is enough, and he does not have to prove his complaint justified. The wife has no corresponding right. A girl has no right to choose her husband; she may be given in marriage by her father to whomever he pleases, and he may even sell her into slavery. No doubt Hebrew women had their own ways of exerting influence on their menfolk; but in the last resort right and power were entirely in masculine hands.

Thirdly, this morality is based on the idea of sexual property-right. A woman is owned, before marriage by her father, after marriage by her husband, to whom the father transfers his right of possession. (The Anglican marriage service, preserving this tradition, says 'Who giveth this woman to be married to this man?', whereas the bridegroom is his own master and does not have to be given away.) This attitude comes out clearly in the Tenth Commandment, where the main items of property are listed, beginning with the house as the most valuable, and proceeding by way of the wife to the slaves and domestic animals. The husband does not belong to the wife in the same way; there is no commandment 'Thou shalt not covet thy neighbour's husband'. The point of view is exclusively male, and the woman figures, like the house, as an object owned, not as a subject of rights and duties. Sexual offences are dealt with as infringements of these rights of ownership. A great value is attached to *female* chastity; but it is clear that this value lies in the exclusive right of possession which chastity confers on the husband. Thus a man who rapes a woman who is married or betrothed (that is, *sexually* owned) is condemned to death. But if the girl is not betrothed he has committed a smaller offence; for since nobody possesses sexual rights over the girl, nobody has lost those rights. The loss is suffered by her father, who is now the owner of a less valuable piece of property, and must therefore be compensated. As for the girl, she is disposed of by being married to her ravisher without regard to her interests or wishes, with only the dubious advantage that he may not thereafter divorce her.

This Hebrew code is plainly devised by men in the interest of men. It is a rather extreme specimen of a type of sexual morality very widespread in human history. There is nothing particularly Jewish about it, and it does not properly represent the customs and attitudes of the Jews of the Christian era, who have been, like their Christian neighbours, a strictly monogamous people whose women hold an influential place in their society.

Patriarchal sex morality is characteristic, not of any particular race of people, but of a particular stage in social development, an early stage of civilisation at which masculine domination of society is especially marked.* Some male dominance exists in every human society, but the degree of this dominance is not everywhere the same. One might expect it to be greatest in savage societies, where life is cruder, poverty and squalor leave little room for gentle and gracious living, and the power of brawn, in which men excel, counts for most. But this is not so. There are indeed primitive communities in which women are persistently bullied and have few rights. But there are others in which women hold their own fairly well in influence and status: some, for instance, in which women own the cultivable land and a man works on his mother-in-law's field; a good many in which a married man has to leave home and live with his wife's people and become in effect a member of her family; many, including a high proportion of the poorest, in which women have equality of rights with men in the making and breaking of marriages. But among these primitive peoples the relative position of women tends to decline as wealth increases. And among ancient civilised peoples the patriarchal system was almost universal, and was most marked among the wealthier and more powerful classes.

The explanation seems to be something like this. In savage society there is so little to go round that nobody is very much richer than his neighbours; there is no room for a class of rich and powerful idlers, or for a class of slaves about whom nobody cares. But civilised society brings into existence marked class differences between rich and poor, powerful and powerless. And the extra wealth and power brought into existence gets into the hands of men. The pursuits which yield large

* The evidence is assembled in E. Westermarck, *History of Human Marriage*, Chapters XXII and XXXII.

returns in wealth and power are male pursuits—technical expertise, long-distance trade, administration and, above all, war and conquest; and most early civilisations were founded on conquest and dominated by warriors. While the woman is tied to her home by the need to care for her children, individual men by conquest and commerce make themselves rich and powerful enough to make other men their servants, and a wide distinction grows up between the upper classes who command and the lower who obey. The wives of the nobility benefit from the successes of their menfolk; they have more comfort and less toil, and they have servants. But they become the dependants of their husbands instead of their partners. The man of property and power stands less in need of his wife's services. He can replace her as a labourer by hired or bought servants, and as a sexual partner by hired or bought slaves, concubines or prostitutes. So he can exact from her a standard of sexual fidelity to which he does not himself conform. He can insist on her chastity while maintaining his own sexual freedom, because there are other classes of women in society who are not required to be chaste. The double standard of sexual morality requires a distinction between two groups of women. Those of the respectable classes, required to be strictly chaste, are to be the mothers of the next generation of dominating males; if they lack freedom and power, they are still treated with respect and courtesy. The others are not 'respectable'; they are personally despised, and their children have an inferior status. But, given the double standard, they are indispensable. St Augustine puts it like this: 'Remove prostitutes from human affairs, and you will pollute everything with lust; set them among honest matrons, and you will dishonour everything with disgrace and turpitude'; clearly recognising that, in a male-dominated society, prostitutes are needed to maintain the honourable woman's standards of chastity; clearly implying also a double standard of morality in which decent society is defiled by the presence of the prostitute, but not by the presence of the men who patronise her.

There is another factor in the situation. A poor man has little to bequeath to his children; a man of wealth and power has much. So, in a society in which there are great differences in inheritable rank, it matters very much whose son you are. The prospect of inheritance binds sons more closely to their fathers and makes them readier to accept paternal authority lest they should lose their inheritance. So wealth and rank enhance the power of the father over the sons, particularly in a fighting society with habits of strict military discipline. (In some fighting aristocracies, including the Roman, the father had the power of life and death over his sons.) The male descendants of men of importance come to be very conscious of their descent; family loyalties, family ties, family reputation are matters of great concern. And the family here means the succession of sons, to whom the inheritance passes, since they alone are able to defend and increase it. In patriarchal society a man belongs to the family into which he is born, a woman to the family into which she marries. (A titled lady showing us round her Stately Home remarked: '*We* came here in 1276', meaning by 'we' the male ancestors of her husband.) Her importance is that she is the mother of the next generation of sons. It has been a regular practice among rich and powerful families to form and strengthen political and business alliances by marrying the daughter of one house to the son of another, of course with little regard to their wishes or mutual compatibility. In India, and in medieval Europe, this was often done when the parties were young children. The Hebrew rule that a widow without sons (daughters are ignored) must marry her husband's brother, and her first son count as the son of the deceased, is aimed at securing the continuance of the family line, and heirs for the family property. In ancient Athens, if a man of property died leaving only a daughter to inherit, the heiress had to marry the next male heir, regardless of age or suitability in other respects, so that the property might not pass out of the family, even though one or other of them might have to divorce their present spouse. In these cases the woman is clearly regarded not as a person whose interests need to be consulted but as a mechanism by which the family is to be perpetuated.

Where the family line is so important, purity of blood is essential. The man with something to bequeath wants to be sure that his heirs are of his own body. So the chastity of the legitimate wife is of supreme importance to him and the family; and there is a sharp distinction between legitimate and illegitimate children. In many savage societies however this is not a matter of importance. A man who practises wife-lending is clearly prepared to treat as his own any children she may have by other fathers. Sometimes much of a man's attention is given, and some of his goods bequeathed, not to his own but to his sister's sons. There are even savage communities in which the fact of physical paternity is not acknowledged at all. But a civilised 'man of family', who has land, livestock, money, a peerage or shares in the family business to hand on, cannot bear that there should be any doubt that his heir is really his son. Here is another source of the great stress on female chastity: the father must be assured of the legitimacy of his wife's children, and to provide them is her principal function. So the bastard is excluded from the presence of the tribal God, the God of Abraham, Isaac and Jacob, that is, the God of a family line of men of property and power.

Patriarchal types of sexual morality were characteristic of ancient civilisations in general—Greek and Roman, Indian, Chinese, Arabian. For Greece, the attitude is expressed by the dramatist Menander, who says: 'The life of a respectable woman is bounded by the street door', and the orator Demosthenes,* who says: 'We keep mistresses for pleasure, concubines for daily attendance on our person, and wives to bear us legitimate children and to be our faithful housekeepers.' The Hindu *Kama Sutra* speaks in the same style: 'When Kama [sexual intercourse] is practised by men of the four castes according to the rules of Holy Writ [i.e. in lawful marriage] with virgins of their own caste, it then becomes a means of acquiring lawful progeny and good fame. . . . On the contrary the practice of Kama with women of the higher castes, and with those previously enjoyed by others, even though they be of the same caste, is prohibited. But the practice of Kama with women of the lower castes, with women excommunicated from their own caste, with public women and with women twice married, is neither enjoined nor prohibited. The object of practising Kama with such women is pleasure only.' And again: 'When a girl becomes marriageable her parents should . . . show her to advantage in society, because she is a kind of merchandise.'

In these ancient cultures a woman was not an independent agent, but was owned by some man. If of the respectable classes, she was forbidden to mate with any man other than her husband, while he was under no such restriction. She could not choose for herself

* Or some contemporary; the authorship is uncertain.

whom she would marry; and she had either no right to divorce, or a very restricted right compared with her husband. There were, of course, plenty of differences in detail. The Hebrew code is exceptional in the severity of its punishments. The provisions for divorce varied from one country and period to another. In Europe, even before the Christian era, a man was allowed only one legitimate wife, whereas Asiatic codes generally permitted several. This matter of polygyny deserves a brief comment. Societies which permit it are a good deal commoner than those which forbid it; but, even where it is permitted, it is usually quite rare. It can occur on a large scale where there is a large surplus of women over men—this is most likely to happen among very warlike peoples with a heavy death-rate among fighting men, the survivors parcelling out the women between them. Polygyny can also be common in a society in which a small group of men are powerful enough to deprive some of the weaker ones of all sexual opportunity; since where the numbers of the sexes are nearly equal, for every man who has two wives there must be another who has none. So 'One man one wife', like 'One man one vote', is a democratic principle, and may expect the support of most ordinary males. Women are not always opposed to polygyny, as the Mormons showed by their success in attracting recruits to their polygynous society. The system can work with a reasonable degree of satisfaction to the wives under certain favourable conditions; for instance, where each woman has her own house or hut with her own children, and the husband visits them in pretty strict rotation, so that each woman gets alternate periods of company and peace. It can also work if the wives are sisters or close friends before marriage; many of the uncivilised peoples permitting polygyny restrict it to the case where the wives are sisters. But outside these special conditions, where there are several wives in one household who have originally been strangers to one another, competition, strife and ill-feeling within the household between the wives and between their respective families are very probable—and the husband, too, gets involved in the trouble. So, given a normal balance of numbers between the sexes, only a very powerful ruling class can make polygyny a common state of affairs. Even in modern Mohammedan countries, though sanctioned by religious tradition, it is rare and tends to be disapproved of.

The patriarchal tradition is to this day dominant in India and the Mohammedan world, and was so in China until the recent revolution. In Europe the tradition has been greatly modified under Christian influence; nevertheless the patriarchal double standard has always been a strong element in the sexual morality even of officially Christian Europe. The English squires in *Tom Jones*, for instance, clearly hold to its main principles: they assume that a girl's husband should be chosen for her by her father; they regard unchastity in a woman as the gravest of faults, but in a man, such as Tom himself, as hardly a fault at all. Even in twentieth-century Europe there is plenty of this attitude of mind surviving. A recent and penetrating book by an Italian about his fellow-countrymen gives this account of the prevalent doctrine on sexual morality. 'What is woman? She was obviously placed on earth to amuse and comfort (her husband). . . . Like all inferior people, she must by every means be kept in her place *for her own sake* above all. . . . She knows practically nothing of her husband's private life. Has he a mistress? Has he two? Does he go from one regular liaison to another or does he have several at the same time? . . . She is only rarely jealous. . . . As for herself, she knows she must be very careful and not so much as look at another man. If she did, she would deserve severe punishment, repudiation, and, frequently enough, death.'* The double standard appears in Italian law, by which adultery is a crime on the part of the woman, but not on the part of the man unless accompanied by scandalous behaviour. A similar discrimination survived in English law until 1923. A striking recent example of the operation of the double standard in this country was the enforced abdication of King Edward VIII, when the government ruled that a woman who had been previously married and divorced was therefore unfit to be Queen, though nobody suggested that unchastity in Edward would be an obstacle to his being King, and there would have been no trouble if he had simply made Mrs Simpson his mistress, after the manner of most of his predecessors. It is notable that this case concerned the aristocracy, where the double standard had been more strongly entrenched. How far it affected the masses is not so certain. One hears that among some lower-class English groups the custom used to exist that a man would not marry a girl until

* L. Barzini, *The Italians*, Chapter XI.

she had become pregnant and so shown herself capable of bearing children.

The influence of the double-standard morality can be traced in the meanings of some of our moral words. A man's 'virtue' is the whole range of his good qualities. But a woman's 'virtue', when the term was still used, meant her chastity and nothing else. The preservation of her husband's (or prospective husband's) sexual rights was so important that it outweighed all her other good and bad qualities. Similarly, a 'good girl', until very recently, meant a chaste girl, whereas a 'good boy' never meant a chaste boy.

Systems of sexual morality, as we have said, are regularly justified by myths. The myth which supports the patriarchal system is a portrayal of the Nature of Woman; it may be found in innumerable disquisitions by male writers from all periods of history. Woman, according to this myth, is inferior to man, not only in muscular strength (which is obvious) but also in intellectual capacity. She is weak-willed and timid, incapable of organising or effectively exer- cising authority. She is emotional and lacking in self-control, frivolous and fickle. She is 'intuitive', which is a polite way of saying that she cannot draw logical inferences but just jumps to conclusions. At her best she is naïve and trusting; at her worst, sly and treacherous. To formulate a theory, to work out a principle of conduct and stick to it, to pursue a plan of action steadfastly and consistently, a man is needed. It is therefore obvious that she needs to be controlled and guided by the more efficient and rational male. Fortunately, this is just what she herself prefers. She does not enjoy freedom and authority; she is only really comfortable when she has a master to rule her and relieve her of responsibility. She even rather likes being bullied—'A woman, a dog and a walnut tree; The more you beat 'em, the better they be' has equivalents in other languages. Her good qualities are patience and gentleness.

> *O woman, in our hours of ease,*
> *Uncertain, coy, and hard to please . . .*
> *When pain and anguish wring the brow,*
> *A ministering angel thou!*
> Walter Scott

When the man returns exhausted from the effort and conflict of the hunt, the plough, the battlefield or the board meeting, his wife is waiting with a smile to hang up his coat, serve him a meal and take his head on her lap with soothing speeches. (Hence nursing, though it is dangerous, dirty and mentally and physically tiring, is held to be a very suitable job for a woman.) Apart from this personal care, her special talents are for entertainment and decoration: she makes up her face, dresses prettily, plays the piano and does the flowers. She has also one physical superiority over the male: she is less sensitive to pain. It follows that hurting a woman doesn't matter so much as hurting a man. (Women have a rival myth that men are a lot of babies who are no good at enduring pain.)

Some versions of the myth also offer an account of the sexual nature of woman. 'The majority of women (happily for society) are not very much troubled with sexual feeling of any kind', wrote a distinguished English doctor of the nineteenth century. A celebrated Italian doctor of the same period reported that 'Woman is naturally and organically frigid.' Since she has little or no sexual appetite, it is no hardship to her to be chaste. Sexual intercourse, which serves to relieve and delight the male, is to her mainly a way of gratifying her husband and obtaining the children whom every woman desires and rejoices in. Moreover, while men are naturally polygamous, desiring variety in their sexual experience, and for the man loving one woman is no bar to desiring others, women are naturally monogamous; the woman who loves one man has no interest in others, and her instinct is to find one man to love and stick to him. Admittedly this description does not apply to all women without exception; but the exceptions are departures from the normal, they are freakish and defective. Clever and intellectual women, bossy and managing women, women with strong sexual appetites, are in their various ways freaks and misfits; they must be given no encouragement in their oddities.

This is not exactly a false picture. It is true enough to its model. But it is not a picture of Woman as she is by nature, always and necessarily. It is a picture of Woman as she has been made by her situation in a male-dominated society; and especially of the woman of the upper classes, sheltered from some of the roughnesses of life, and with enough spare time for the piano and the flowers. Women conform to this pattern to the extent to which they have responded to their training for a predetermined role. We all know by now that women are capable of doing many things and displaying many qualities of character for which they have had no opportunity under the masculine domination of most of human history. The feminine character in a people at a given period is partly determined by innate characteristics and partly by training and opportunity; women develop those characteristics that they are expected and encouraged to develop and are rewarded for displaying. This indoctrination into the female role begins very early in childhood. Wherever men count for more than women, the little girl learns this fact in infancy. Her future career is pointed out to her in the very toys given her and the games she is invited to play; nobody gives a boy a doll or a girl a football.

All the same, there *are* great differences in physical constitution between boys and girls, and it would be extraordinary if these had no effect on temperament and capacities. To assess the value of the patriarchal myth about the nature of woman, we have to know how much of the difference between the average man and the average woman is due to innate constitution, and how much to training. This is very difficult to find out, because it is impossible to get rid entirely of the influence of training. Some things, however, are clear. It is clear that there is a constitutional difference between the sexes in physical strength. The average woman cannot compete with the average man in running, lifting, throwing, sawing, digging, wrestling, anything which needs muscular power and the short-term expenditure of a great deal of energy. Nevertheless, when it comes to physical endurance, keeping going for long periods without rest, doing without food, withstanding cold, women often turn out the tougher sex; and given equal conditions they tend to live longer than men—girl babies in particular are less delicate than boys. There is a biological reason for this extra toughness of the female. If she were not hard-wearing and able to stand up to severe pain without collapsing, she would be unable to endure childbirth, which is often agonising and protracted and was even more so before anaesthetics and modern relaxation methods. It is often said among women that if men had to bear the children they would not be so eager to have families; it may be that they would not be capable of undergoing childbirth without some modification to their nervous systems. A woman may also have to recover quickly from childbirth in order to nurse and tend the young baby. She must be able to carry out her duties when short of sleep, because in the early weeks of life children have to be fed during the night, and often pass through a period when they repeatedly cry in the night and have to be cared for. Similarly, a woman sometimes has to be able to survive on little food so that she can care for her family in times of emergency, giving up part of her own meals to them. In the European wartime shortages of our own lifetime it has been common for women to give up their meagre rations of meat, eggs or butter to their children and husbands.

Another plain fact is that the intellectual superiority of men, where it exists, is a result of opportunity and not of natural endowment. Given similar educational opportunities (for which in Britain they have had to wait until the present century), girls on the average do as well as boys. It seems safe to say that the talent for understanding, organising and planning is as widely distributed among girls as among boys, and if girls fail to develop it to the same extent, it is because they lack incentive and opportunity. (In the working-class household the woman is the manager.) Women make competent doctors, journalists, business managers. If they rarely reach the top, this is due partly to the constant opposition of the entrenched males, partly to the diversion of their own interests to home and children. Apart from professional sport and heavy manual labour (which in the modern world is of diminishing importance) there is no occupation in which the abler women are not ahead of the majority of the men. (The actual division of labour in a community usually has little to do with the relative capacities of the sexes; it was not because of their muscular inferiority that women were given such jobs as washing blankets and scrubbing floors. The tasks entrusted to women have been those that could be done at home, without moving very far from the small children whom they have always had to look after.)

About innate sex differences in temperament it is harder to speak with confidence. We are probably safe in crediting (or debiting) the male with a greater inborn aggressiveness—this is pretty well universal among all species of mammals. Man is psychologically as well as physically a more ready and formidable fighter than woman. A mature woman is subject to variations of mood connected with the menstrual cycle, which men escape. And she is probably more susceptible than a man to the appeal of babies and young children, the small, weak and helpless, to the longing for some living thing to cherish and pet. There is some evidence of a submissive tendency that is commoner among women than among men; there are women who enjoy yielding to male domination, who rush to humour the caprices of their masters and may even like being beaten. This tendency probably originates in the passive, receptive role of the woman in sexual intercourse and may spread throughout her attitudes to husband or lover. Men regard it as a female excellence and have tended to demand it as of right. Some male psychiatrists maintain that women who are without it must be maladjusted, suffering from 'feminine protest', refusing their female role in life. The yielding and receptive attitude of women in love-making is a normal phenomenon over which they have little control. But the carrying over of this attitude into everyday relations with husband, lover, male relatives or colleagues and superiors at work, is by no means universal, nor is there any reason why it should be. A woman, once out of her husband's bed, may have children to tend whose welfare while they are young is often more important to her than any wish of his. Up to the age of menstruation girls are often as bold and disinclined to submission as boys, and the same is true of women after the menopause. In between, some women are by nature submissive, others have been trained to submissiveness, and some are never anything but independent and rebellious, whether or not they have the opportunity for showing this. Many feel within themselves a conflict between the old Eve who enjoys waiting on Adam hand and foot and then being trampled on, and the impatient individualist who says 'Why should I? Who does he think he is?' There may well be as many women who dominate their husbands as men who dominate their wives; the outward appearance of a marriage can be utterly deceptive on this point. As regards clinging tendencies, possessiveness, love of gossip, shrinking from responsibility, treacherousness, feeling for detail, all characteristics supposed by men to be especially feminine, everyday observation suggests that they are as common among men. The old notion of womanly temperament is thus seen to be at least an exaggeration; although women are in general less aggressive than men, more susceptible to the appeal of the small and the weak to be cherished, more variable in mood and more yielding in love, other temperamental differences seem likely to be the effects of conditioning for the social role allotted to them.

As to sexual desires, it is of course absurd to deny that women have them. Many women are indeed frigid, but their frigidity is not due to an initial absence of sexual appetite. A girl may become frigid if her introduction to sex has been painful, frightening or otherwise disagreeable. But much more often frigidity is due to the way she has been brought up. If she has been given no information about sex, and it has never been plainly mentioned in her presence, but only obliquely hinted at in a tone of anxiety and disgust; if any interest in the sexual parts, any curiosity about physical intimacy has been severely condemned as naughty and unladylike, she may become unwilling to attempt sexual relations and unable to enjoy them. But even when this anti-sex training is effective, it does not destroy the sexual impulse, which is likely to take the form of masturbation. The frequency of masturbation in women★ is the clearest evidence that the sexual impulse is there, however much it may be checked by fear and shame.

Nevertheless, for women growing up in any imaginable human society, there are differences in the character of the desire as between the two sexes. As a rule, the woman's desires are more slowly aroused. A man may be ready to jump into bed and get busy a few minutes after meeting a pretty girl for the first time; a woman usually needs a period of preparation and courting. The mere sight of a desirable male is not enough to set her juices flowing, as the mere sight of a desirable female may be enough to give a man an erection. The woman's desire is less immediately insistent. Also, it is less immediately recognisable. A man who is amorous knows exactly what he wants, and he also knows when he has got it; there is no possibility of mistaking sexual desire for something else. The feeling is exactly and sharply located in one place. He wants to penetrate the woman and emit semen. When he succeeds in doing this, he feels pleasure;

★ 62 per cent in Kinsey's sample; other investigations give over 70 per cent.

having done it, his desire promptly dies down, and his inclination, as like as not, is to turn over and go to sleep. The woman is less clearly aware what it is she wants. To have any responses at all, she needs to be stimulated by the man; her responses are more various and more diffused over different parts of her body. Orgasm in the male is definite and unmistakable, precisely located, and invariable; without it he cannot take his part in procreation. Orgasm in the female may or may not take place when she mates. If it does, it may occur externally (clitoral) or internally (vaginal) at different depths and intensities. It is said that the deeper, internal orgasm of the vagina is the kind in which a woman herself is more emotionally involved, whereas the surface clitoral orgasm, more sharply exciting, can be brought about by skill alone. Most women have not learned this distinction, and so a woman may be in doubt whether she has had an orgasm, or a 'proper' orgasm. Many go through a long married life without ever achieving one of any kind. But this makes no difference to their ability to conceive children. A woman's responses are slower, so that to give her satisfaction usually takes more time than the male needs to do his biological job and get his own satisfaction. But this delayed response, once aroused, can be as strong as the man's and more persistent; she is ready for more when he is already tired and sated. Thus she is much less certain than he of satisfaction in mating. Also, although girls become sexually mature at an earlier age than boys, their sexual desires develop more slowly. Thus, quite apart from social conditioning, there are two kinds of cause which make female sexual desire less imperious than that of the male. It is more slowly aroused, more dependent on external stimulation, less explicit in its demands. And it is much more liable to be damped down by the failure to gain enjoyment from intercourse. It is very common to find women in early middle age who have had enough of the whole business, while their husbands' appetites are still hot; and this can be a cause of serious marital disturbance. But it is not easy to decide how far this is due to a constitutional weakness or transience of sexual desire, and how far it is due to a disappointing experience of sexual relations.

It is, then, false that any woman altogether lacks sexual desire, though some women may fail to recognise or acknowledge it. If a woman fails to enjoy mating, it is not because she is constitutionally incapable of it. It may be the effect of a reluctance, a shrinking from the experience, which she has been taught to entertain; or it may be the effect of a maladjustment between her requirements and the habits or capacities of her mate.

As for the contrast between the naturally polygamous male and the naturally monogamous female, this also, in so far as it is real, is the result of training. If a woman has no interest in or desire for any other man than her husband, this is not just because of her sexual or emotional nature. It is because her attachment to her husband is socially approved, and she can entertain it without shame or reluctance; because also it is an attachment to security, support, affection, status, whereas all these things are jeopardised if she forms attachments elsewhere. It is an effect of the double-standard morality, not a cause. A man dares to look at other women; a woman in a double-standard society does not dare to look at other men. But if her husband fails to give her security, affection, and status, she *will* look elsewhere. And if it becomes safe for her to indulge her taste for variety, she will often show that she shares this taste with men (there were plenty of examples of this even when the double standard was strong, in women who were not dependent on men, such as successful actresses and reigning queens). In fact, a woman is more likely than a man to get variety of experience if she changes her partner, since the man mainly determines the character of the intercourse.

Nevertheless there is a difference between male and female sexuality which is relevant to this point, and which may have a biological basis. 'Man's love is of man's life a thing apart, 'Tis woman's whole existence.' A man can more easily than a woman detach his sexual life from the rest of his interests and sentiments, take his matings as casual incidents to be experienced and forgotten. He can more easily take a woman without his feelings being involved. With women this is not so easy. They are usually more choosy whom they accept; women prepared to take any man who is available are much rarer than the corresponding type of man. The reasons for this may still be largely cultural—a woman who takes a mate commits herself more completely and therefore requires to be satisfied about his suitability and her own feelings. But there are two biological factors which also make a difference. One is that a woman is deeply committed not only socially but physically; the consequences of a single sexual act for her may last a lifetime, so that it is harder for her to give herself casually. The other is that the female sexual arousal, more gradual and diffused than the male, may from the start be more closely bound up with emotional responses, and so less easily separated from her interest as a person in the man who arouses her. In the sexual act the male, the initiator and the more active performer, can easily think only of himself and regard the woman as a tool, a convenience or a victim. If a woman feels that much indifference to her man, she is likely to lose the power of physically responding to him, though she may simulate it. So in matters of love men are apt to look for pretty faces, and women for affection.

So there is something in the patriarchal picture of the nature of woman, but not much; certainly not enough to justify either the general subordination of women, or discrimination in sexual opportunity. A training which aims at inducing frigidity amongst all women who hope to be regarded as respectable deprives the woman, and to a smaller degree her husband, of opportunities of enjoyment and means of endearment to one another. The man may escape his deprivation by having available to him other women less respectably brought up. The woman is deprived in any case.

But whatever we think of its theories, the double-standard sex morality no longer finds much support in countries of a modern standard of civilisation. Industrial society liquidates the patriarch. It abolishes slavery and serfdom, the purchase and inheritance of 'souls'. It introduces universal education, free competition for profits, jobs, seats in parliament, and breaks down the rigid distinction between the nobility and gentry and the common people. In industrial competition the firms that prevail are those that give a man a job because he has the right technical qualifications, and not because he is somebody's cousin. Above all, industrialisation squeezes out domestic crafts and draws the women outside the home, to make them wage-earners in their own right instead of dependants of the men. Once a woman can earn her own living she cannot be compelled to accept masculine dictation. An industrial society has got to educate its girls and give them openings for careers, because in competition

with its rivals it cannot afford to neglect their skills. So the pater-
familias loses his grip over wife and daughters, and over his sons too,
since their chances in life come to depend on school grades and
examinations and not on their father's influence. In such a social
background a demand is bound to arise for equality of rights for
women. And, Freud or no Freud, women will claim and achieve
something nearer to equality, not only in careers and votes and entry
to universities, but in sexual liberty and the right to sexual satisfaction.

3

The Puritan Attitude

In the patriarchal system of sex morality, it is taken for granted that sexual intercourse is one of the good things of life, an experience well worth having and enjoying, for men at any rate. It is good for them to marry and produce children to succeed them. The importance attached to the family line leads to marriage being regarded as a duty as well as a pleasure. The bachelor is evading his responsibilities to his ancestors, who have a right to the perpetuation of their line. (In many patriarchal societies, notably the Chinese, ancestors were objects of worship, powerful and revered figures demanding a succession of descendants to do them honour.) The man who does not marry is also evading his duties to his relatives and to his tribe or nation, which requires a steady supply of citizens and fighting men. In patriarchal society he is regarded with suspicion and hostility, as a shirker or queer. As for the women, they are married off as a matter of course; that is what they are for.

But among the elements in our own moral thinking there is included a tradition of a very different kind: a tradition which regards sex itself with suspicion and hostility and which, so far from despising the celibate, views him as a superior type. For this tradition sex, if not exactly evil, is yet to some degree tainted and dangerous. Far from being an essential element in the good life, it is to be avoided as much as possible, to be indulged in sparingly and warily, a thing to be ashamed of and to keep quiet about. This attitude to sex is associated with ascetic religion, and in Europe has been almost entirely of Christian origin. It cannot be called *the* Christian view of sex; there is no such thing, for there are considerable differences about sex morality between individual Christians and between different churches—for instance, the Catholic prohibitions of divorce and of the marriage of priests are not accepted by either Protestant or Orthodox Churches. What we shall call the puritan attitude to sexual morality is not and never has been the attitude of all Christians. But it seems to have predominated in the Church during the later Roman Empire, a decisive period for the formation of Christian doctrine, some features of it are still officially promulgated by the Church of Rome, and it exercises an influence on Christian thinking everywhere.

Christian ideas about sex have not been derived to any great extent from the teaching of Jesus. The only clear statement about sexual morality recorded in the Gospels is the one occurring in *Matthew*, XIX, 3–9, and V, 31–2, *Mark*, X, 2–12, and *Luke*, XVI, 18. This contains a clear condemnation of divorce at the husband's pleasure, but the texts are not agreed as to whether Jesus made an exception of divorce for adultery. The authoritative text for Christian doctrine regarding sex has been St Paul's *First Epistle to the Corinthians*. The relevant passages are these.

> It is well for a man not to touch a woman. But because of the temptation to immorality, each man should have his own wife and each woman her own husband. The husband should give to the wife her conjugal rights, and likewise the wife to her husband. For the wife does not rule over her own body, but the husband does; likewise the husband does not rule over his own body, but the wife does. Do not refuse one another, except perhaps by agreement for a season, that you may devote yourselves to prayer; but then come together again, lest Satan tempt you through lack of self-control. . . . I wish that all were as I myself am. But each has his own special gift from God, one of one kind and one of another. To the unmarried and the widows I say that it is well for them to remain single as I do. But if they cannot exercise self-control, they should marry. For it is better to marry than to be aflame with passion. To the married I give charge, not I but the Lord, that the wife should not separate from her husband (but if she does, let her remain

single or else be reconciled to her husband), and that the husband should not divorce his wife. . . . If any brother has a wife who is an unbeliever, and she consents to live with him, he should not divorce her. If any woman has a husband who is an unbeliever, and he consents to live with her, she should not divorce him. . . . But if the unbelieving partner desires to separate, let it be so; in such a case the brother or sister is not bound. . . . Are you bound to a wife? Do not seek to be free. Are you free from a wife? Do not seek marriage. But if you marry, you do not sin, and if a girl marries, she does not sin. Yet those who marry will have worldly troubles, and I would spare you that. . . . The unmarried man is anxious about the affairs of the Lord, how to please the Lord; but the married man is anxious about worldly affairs, how to please his wife. And the unmarried woman or girl is anxious about the affairs of the Lord, how to be holy in body and spirit; but the married woman is anxious about worldly affairs, how to please her husband [*I Corinthians*, VII].

Any man who prays or prophesies with his head covered dishonours his head, but any woman who prays or prophesies with her head unveiled dishonours her head—it is the same as if her head were shaven. . . . For a man ought not to cover his head, since he is the image and glory of God; but woman is the glory of man. (For man was not made from woman, but woman from man. . . . Nevertheless in the Lord woman is not independent of man nor man of woman.) [*I Corinthians*, XI].

The women should keep silence in the churches. For they are not permitted to speak, but should be subordinate, as even the law says. If there is anything they desire to know, let them ask their husbands at home [*I Corinthians*, XIV].

Two things are notable about this. One is that St Paul, like all other men of his period, accepts the principle of male superiority. Women are to be members of the Church, but subordinate members, whose voices are not to be heard; and the married woman is to be obedient to her husband. Probably Christianity did not at first make much difference to the relative position of women. The attitude of Paul, and of the early Church, to the subjection of women was like their attitude to slavery. He urges husbands to be kind to their wives, and slave-owners to their slaves; but he also upholds the right of both husbands and slave-owners to be obeyed, and he does not challenge either the institution of slavery or the dominance of the male. This principle of male dominance has remained attached to Christianity throughout its history; now, while women are being admitted to positions of responsibility and authority in business, the professions, politics and the arts, the male monopoly of power in the Churches remains almost completely unbroken.

The other notable feature of Paul's views is of great importance. He maintains that, while faithful marriage is superior to fornication, and is indeed a good thing in itself, complete abstinence from sex is a still better thing. Paul gives this as his own opinion, and not as the teaching of Jesus (who was indeed celibate himself, but is not said to have required celibacy from his followers). His reason seems to be that married people are concerned with pleasing each other rather than pleasing God. It was this view, perhaps derived from the authority of Paul, and certainly defended by appeals to that authority, which became prevalent among the leaders of Christian thought in the time of the 'fathers of the Church', when Christian doctrine was being systematised.

The puritan doctrine developed by the Fathers, particularly by St Augustine, and sustained throughout the Middle Ages, has as its foundation the principle that sexual intercourse is in itself unclean. 'The ministerial office', says St Ambrose, 'must be kept *pure* and *unspotted*, and must not be *defiled* by sexual intercourse.'* According to St Thomas Aquinas, 'The shamefulness of concupiscence that always accompanies the marriage act is . . . a punishment inflicted for the first sin, inasmuch as the lower powers and members do not obey reason.' Augustine associated sexual intercourse with the fall of man, speaking as though our liability to erotic passion was a feature, even the central feature, of the debasement of human nature resulting from the sin of Adam. In the garden of Eden, he supposed, sex as we experience it could not have occurred. 'Far be it from us to think that in marriages which would have taken place in Paradise the genitals would have been excited by the ardour of lust and not by the bidding

* *De Officiis*, 1, 50.

of the will.'* Clearly what worries him about sex is its involuntary, impassioned nature, its capacity to carry us away. To be sexually excited, and to go on to intercourse, is like being taken hold of by a physical, animal power that is not yourself. It is this subservience to animal appetite which Augustine found humiliating about sex; and he imagined that man's inability to direct his sexual urges voluntarily was the result of his imperfect, fallen nature.

If sex is unclean, the highest human state must be one in which it is renounced altogether. All those who aimed at being in a special sense 'religious', monks, nuns and hermits who wished to devote themselves to God in a more than ordinary fashion, were required to live without it. Improving stories were told of how this or that saint spent his wedding night converting his bride to a lifetime of holy celibacy. What of the clergy, the religious leaders and teachers of the people, who might be expected to aim at a specially high standard of purity? At first celibacy was demanded only of bishops, as is still the rule in the Eastern Church; in early times, married men appointed as bishops were required to separate from their wives. After some centuries of controversy, the rule of celibacy was imposed on all clergy of the Western Church, though only the Roman Catholics still adhere to it.

The holiest form of life, then, is one without sexual gratification. But not everybody is equal to the demands of the celibate life. For those who are not, marriage was instituted as a second best, not so good as abstinence but better than promiscuity, as 'a remedy against sin, and to avoid fornication; that such persons as have not the gift of continency might marry, and keep themselves undefiled members of Christ's body', as the Anglican marriage service puts it. The rather disgusting practice of mating is rendered respectable and even meritorious when it is used for a worthy purpose. Aquinas says: 'If the motive for the marriage act be a virtue, whether of justice, that they may render the debt, or of religion, that they may beget children for the worship of God, it is meritorious. But if the motive be lust, it is a sin.'† Sexual intercourse is justified by its primary purpose of the procreation of children, for the continuance of the species and the expansion of the Christian Church to the greater glory of God. But

* *De Ordine*, II, 4 [12].
† *Summa Theologiae*, Supp., XLI, 4.

a secondary purpose is also allowed: to quote the Anglican service again, 'the mutual society, help and comfort that the one ought to have of the other'. Sex in marriage serves a good end in so far as the partners therein fulfil their contractual obligations and strengthen their mutual enjoyment and affection. Under these conditions it is not only permissible but holy. The doctrine that sex is unclean is oddly combined with the doctrine that marriage is a sacrament, in rather the same way in which the doctrine that government is a remedy against sin, and would not exist in a perfect human society, is combined with the doctrine that the authority of rulers is sacred and comes from God. Marriage is a sacrament, because it is both a physical representation of the love between Christ and his Church, and also a means whereby the grace of God may reach the wedded pair. Its sacramental nature is dependent on the proper performance of the marriage ceremony, and on the intention of the couple to keep their vows, to produce children who will be brought up for the service of God, and to be faithful to one another. It does not depend on their feelings towards one another; marriage is no less a sacrament because there is no love between the partners.

But while sex in marriage can be excused and even sanctified, it is still not to be encouraged. The tendency of puritan thought throughout is to multiply restrictions and obstacles to sexual gratification, and to regard abstinence even on the permitted occasions as meritorious. All sexual gratification except between husband and wife is of course completely forbidden: adultery, fornication, homosexuality, bestiality, masturbation. But even within marriage one must not make love too often. 'He who loves his wife too ardently', says Aquinas, 'is an adulterer.' Married couples were encouraged to abstain on Sundays, Fridays and various other holy days. The Western Church refused to countenance divorce with the right of remarriage for any cause, though it allowed separation from an adulterous or unbelieving spouse on condition of remaining celibate. For a long time the Church strongly disapproved of remarriage for the widowed. In the same spirit, the obstacles to lawful marriage arising from blood-relationship were multiplied during the Middle Ages: first the table of prohibited degrees was extended to include cousins up to the seventh degree, then godfathers and godmothers (being notionally equivalent to fathers and mothers) and all their relatives were added. Former marriage or betrothal to a relative also operated as a bar, so that it was difficult for a man living in a small place to find among his female acquaintances any girl who was not banned as a possible wife for one reason or another. (This procedure had one odd result. Since the prohibitions were so extensive, if a man wished to be rid of his wife he could generally find some ground for arguing that the marriage had been invalid, leaving him free to repudiate her and marry again; so that while the medieval Western Church would not allow divorce for any reason, it could be induced, at least by influential persons, to pronounce decrees of nullity which served the same purpose.)

To the patriarchal moralist, women, when kept firmly in their place, can be useful and enjoyable adjuncts to the masculine good life. By contrast, the puritan attitude to women is grudging and suspicious. They appear to him in the guise of Eve the temptress, as a threat to his safety and purity; in fact, he is scared of them. 'Each of you', says Tertullian, 'is also an Eve. . . . You are the devil's gateway . . . the first transgressors of the divine law. . . . How easily you destroyed Man, the image of God!'* A woman ought not to make herself attractive to men, since this might arouse their sexual desires, which, the puritan assumes, is always to be avoided. 'Even natural beauty ought to be destroyed by concealment and neglect, since it is dangerous to those who look upon it' (Tertullian again).† It is evident that the world of the Fathers was still a man's world, in which women carried the blame even for the appetites of the men.

The counterpart to this fear and dislike of female sexuality was the cult of virginity.‡ Virginity itself was regarded as a woman's greatest merit, and this sentiment gained expression in the worship of the virgin mother of God. It became an accepted tradition, despite the contrary evidence of Scripture, that St Mary not only was a virgin when she gave birth to Jesus, but remained a virgin all her life. So it became possible by means of a single image to honour motherhood and to disparage the act which makes motherhood possible.

* *De Cultu Fem.*, I, I.
† *op. cit.*, II, 2.
‡ 'I praise marriage and wedlock,' said St Jerome, 'but only because they produce virgins.'

The idea that there is something unclean or shameful about sex is not confined to puritans, or to Christians. It is fairly common in primitive religious and magical thinking. One meets it in the notion (found in the Old Testament) that a woman who is menstruating or has just borne a child is 'unclean'. In some religious cults people may be forbidden to enter a temple or holy place immediately after mating. Or mating may be forbidden on specially momentous occasions—a harvest, a military expedition, a religious ceremony—to which it might convey some kind of contamination. We may see in the same light the rules existing in some cultures that particular priests or priestesses must be celibate, either permanently or on ceremonial occasions; the Vestal Virgins of Rome, dedicated to abstinence from sex as part of their service to the goddess, are a famous example.

The association between sex and uncleanness is also a common element in present-day attitudes. A 'filthy postcard' is one which portrays the sexual act or the nude body. 'Dirty' jokes are jokes about sex (most of them expect to get their laughs merely by referring to sex without needing to be funny as well). 'Dirty' language covers references to mating along with references to excretion. Indeed, the bodily organs concerned with sex and with excretion being either the same, or very close together, no doubt one source of the notion that sex is dirty lies in its association with other bodily functions which are dirty in a more literal sense. But this cannot be much of the story. The belief that sex is shameful, impure, obscene (that is, to be kept hidden and not shown, discussed or even referred to in public) is clearly not derived from simple inspection of this attractive and enjoyable experience. It is in the main a consequence of training. It is felt most strongly by those who have been most effectively taught in childhood to restrain the expression of their sexual feelings and impulses. Now, some restraint of this kind is necessary, and is found in all human societies; restraint of sexual impulses is as necessary to harmonious living together as restraint of aggression. But people, and communities, differ in the persistence and severity with which they reprove children for handling and stimulating their own sexual organs and for making sexual advances to one another. And children differ in the extent to which they respond to these reproofs by developing feelings of guilt about their sexual nature. Puritans are people with vigorous consciences, who have responded to sexual and other restraints by developing a strong sense of shame; it is this sense of shame which motivates the longing for *purity* above all else. That indiscriminate, unrestrained sex is wrong or sinful is a lesson that everybody has to learn. But a training which, in order to teach this, produces the conviction that all sex is shameful, overshoots its mark. It is as though, in order to make people ashamed of working on the Lord's Day, we had got into their heads the idea that it is rather indecent to work at all; as though, while trying to prevent our children from growing into gluttons, we had scared them into the conviction that one ought to try to live without eating.

Women are more ready than men to accept the disparagement of sex as filthy. They are in the first place more strictly controlled and more sternly warned against sexual misdemeanours or forwardness. And when they come to experience intercourse, they may often fail to get any pleasure from it, because of their own reluctance or the selfishness or clumsiness of their husbands. If a woman fails to enjoy the sexual act, it will be to her simply a disgusting and disagreeable masculine habit, leading to the discomforts of pregnancy and the pangs of childbirth; and, despite the patriarchal myth, there are plenty of women who dislike even their own children and find motherhood no recompense but an additional burden. This distaste for intercourse (and perhaps for the whole male sex for persistently indulging in the repulsive practice) they convey to their daughters, and the pattern is likely to be repeated over the generations.

Male puritanism is not so easily understood. A man seldom fails to find sex in some degree enjoyable. But he may also find it disagreeable. Perhaps from physical causes he is unable to put up a good performance in bed and satisfy his woman. Perhaps from psychological causes (such as a too intense attachment to his mother) he is unable to give his affection along with his embraces, and feels emotionally unsatisfied. Or perhaps it is the violence of his own lusts, the element of cruelty often present in male sexuality, the vision of himself as a wolf pursuing and devouring a reluctant woman, forcing himself upon her against her will (which happens often enough in marriage) that disgusts him with this part of his own nature. Or, if he has been unable to contain his desires and has got his sex from prostitutes, the character of these encounters, furtive, mercenary, with no liking or respect on either side, may have left a permanently nasty taste in his mouth. Some puritans are libertines who have become disgusted with their own frivolity.

These are all reasons why some individuals may find sex disagreeable or even disgusting. They are not good reasons for holding that sexual intercourse is shameful in itself, for all people in all circumstances. What reasons can be given for this opinion?

One kind of reason may be found in religious asceticism. Asceticism is a view of life present to some extent in all the great religions. It is more characteristic of Hinduism and Buddhism than of Christianity, but it dominated the Christian Church at the time when sexual puritanism became incorporated into Christian doctrine. The ascetic is a person whose dominant aim in life is to be holy, to be like God, to be united with God. His way of achieving this goal is the way of renunciation—to detach himself from every 'worldly' interest and activity, to deny himself and take up his cross. Holiness is conceived as something different from and opposed to worldliness, involving a different attitude of mind, a different mode of experiencing and enjoying from that of ordinary people, a state of mind which can scarcely be described to the uninitiated because there is nothing in their experience to compare it with. Now concentration on God, and on the deeper, purer self, competes with concentration on food, work, sport, social success, beauty for the eye or the ear, all the other enthusiasms and gratifications of unregenerate man. It is not that these things are not good, but they are a lower good, to be renounced for the sake of the highest, the pearl of great price for which a man should be ready to give all that he has. Self-denial is the way of salvation.

From this point of view the pleasures of the ordinary sensual life are to be renounced because, being delightful, they distract men from the pursuit of a greater joy. Sex is one of the worldly pleasures which are to be renounced. It takes a conspicuous place among them because it is particularly insistent, absorbing and distracting. A man meaning to conquer himself must above all conquer this. Moreover, sex has beyond all other common human experiences the power to exalt, to produce ecstasy, to give people the sense of being carried beyond themselves to a higher level of feeling—not, of course, when it is a mere physical detumescence, but when it is associated with love of and delight in another person. In this way sex rivals religion as sport, politics or money-making rarely can. The very language of intense religious passion is notably like that of intense erotic passion. High art can also provide supreme moments for those who fully appreciate it. But the arts can easily be combined with or made subservient to either religion or love, whereas love and religion are not so easily united. Sex, then, appears as a specially strong obstacle to the full devotion which the 'religious' wish to give to God. The conflict between sexual and religious passion seems to be a genuine fact of human experience.*

Still, when a man in pursuit of 'enlightenment' or the mystical vision renounces sex, this is only part of a wholesale renunciation of worldly things. It goes along with the surrender of comfort, financial security, power, status, good food, companionship, entertainment of all kinds, cleanliness (some medieval saints were famous for the abundance of their lice); it is part of a complete mortification of the flesh and the social sentiments. Whether the experiences achieved by those, or some of those, who renounce the world are worth the sacrifice, it is not for us inexperienced ones to determine. We can however point out that a life of this kind is not a possible model for general imitation. Even if everyone were capable of living in this way and achieving mystical experiences, communities of ascetics are neither self-supporting nor self-reproducing. Whatever they achieve in the way of personal purity and exaltation, they usually do it on the charity of more worldly types; and even St Jerome had to concede that it takes married people to provide the next generation of monks and nuns. The excellences of the mystic way, whatever they may be, supply no reason for believing that celibacy, poverty and lousiness are good things for those whose aims are different, those who do not make the total renunciation but have to live and do jobs in 'the world'.

What is there to be said against sexual enjoyment as a part of ordinary life in 'the world'? The case against it is framed in terms of a

* J. D. Unwin's *Sex and Culture* produces much evidence to show that, in communities where sex is under little restraint, there is only a slight development of religious thought.

distinction between the higher and the lower nature of man. Our lower nature is that which we share with the other animals, the life of physical appetite and sensual enjoyment. Our higher nature is peculiar to our species; it is the exercise of understanding, imagination, forethought and the determined pursuit of ideal aims. The only life worth living for man, it is argued, is that according to our higher nature. We must exert our talents and our will-power to the full, trying to achieve the greatest feats of strength and skill, of intellectual understanding or artistic creation, that are within our power. The true destiny and happiness of man lies in doing and achieving, and in perfecting his own capacities for achievement. Work is better than pastimes, and the earnest pastimes involving physical or intellectual effort are better than the indolent pastimes of gambling, spectatorship and lolling on the beach. This good life involves the subjugation of the lower nature, the self of passion, appetite and sensual pleasure. Eating tasty food, drinking intoxicating drinks, sleeping on soft beds, idling in pleasant surroundings on a sunny day are pleasures of this kind. But sex is the most intense of the sensual pleasures, and of them all it is the likeliest to dominate our thought and will, to become a master-passion which crushes our interest in higher things. The more of our time and interest we devote to these lower pleasures, the less we have left for the higher. So there must be a constant struggle to prevent them from getting control of us. We must actually avoid the tastiest meals in case we become too fond of our bellies; we must avoid comfortable chairs and motor transport lest we become too flabby and idle to walk and exert ourselves. We must avoid anything that turns our minds to sensual enjoyment—dancing, love songs, romantic stories, the wearing of attractive clothes. It is even worthwhile to conceal the enjoyableness of sex or alcohol if this will tempt fewer people to be lechers or drunkards.

At its most extreme, the puritan doctrine treats self-denial as a first principle of morality, extols the value of suffering, and despises any kind of spontaneous enjoyment. This attitude is sometimes supported by painting a picture of a mean and vindictive God who demands that his creatures shall earn his favour painfully and enjoys taking it out of them if they manage to achieve a little happiness. This is not Christianity; even Augustine argued against the Manichaean view that everything to do with the body is evil. But the suspicion of enjoyment, especially bodily enjoyment, has influenced the thinking and feeling of many Christians. It is important to realise that the puritanical anti-sex outlook of the Fathers grew up in an age of insecurity and decline, when barbarous invaders were tearing asunder the Roman peace and Roman civilisation, and in each generation the life of man was poorer, less secure, less comfortable than in the generation before. In such an age, the man practised in self-denial had an advantage. Having little to hope for in ordinary life, men turned more readily and more realistically to desert hermitages and mountain monasteries to find in contemplation what was no longer to be found in material prosperity or secure personal relations. Knowing this, we are better able to appreciate and sympathise with these grim ancients; but we have the less reason to follow their advice in an age of progress and hope, when there is reward for effort in worldly activity.

There is, however, another kind of puritanism not so extreme. Without believing in a jealous God, or even a God of any kind, without supposing that there is any virtue or any necessary purifying power in suffering (which depraves men as often as it improves them), one may still hold that the best chances of happiness in this world belong to the man who cultivates his 'higher nature'. Happiness will not be best attained by following physical impulse and pursuing the biggest thrill; it will require the mastery of the passions. The deepest and most dependable satisfactions will be those gained by the man who does something exacting with his whole heart, with all his skill and attention (it may be studying chemistry, playing Bach, climbing mountains, or organising a business), and without much concern for his physical comfort.

If this is the best kind of human life, does it require the sacrifice of sensual enjoyments in general, or sexual enjoyment in particular? The plausibility of the puritan case depends on taking sex as a mere physical sensation like eating and drinking, only more intense. If this is the way one takes it (as Augustine seems to have done), then sex seems a poor thing on which to lavish one's energy and interest. It may be said against the sensualist, as against the glutton, that he would do well to find himself a higher aim in life, something giving more scope to understanding, taste, sympathy. Even the sensualist can reply that he practises an art in the giving and receiving of pleasure by no means to be despised, an art superior to the chef's inasmuch as sexual pleasures outdo the pleasures of the table, and moreover improve when reciprocally given. Those who have no particular talent for music or the visual arts may find in sexual activity their best expression of sensuous delight and appreciation.

But sex need not be taken in this way, as a mere physical titillation. It can also be an expression of love between the partners. Those who disparage sex also disparage marital love. And it is not so easy to maintain that this also belongs to the lower part of human nature. When St Paul complains that whereas the single may care for the Lord's business the married care for one another, what justifies him in counting the care of married people for one another as 'worldly', and presuming that there must be a conflict between pleasing your spouse and pleasing God? Why should one not please God by making a happy and successful marriage? It is clear that what Paul here disparages is not sex, but love; it is not their cohabiting with one another, but their trying to please one another, that he sees as a hindrance to the married couple's love of God. Now, it is true that for a man with a vocation, whether it is religious, like Paul's, or artistic, scientific, political or whatever else, marriage may be a hindrance. If he falls in love with a woman, she will tend to become the centre of his life. He will be worrying about her health and happiness instead of getting on with his life-work; he will find his greatest joy in her company, her collaboration, her embrace. If also he has the management of a household on his shoulders, if he has to provide for the welfare and future careers of his children and deal with the financial, material and emotional problems inseparable from family life, he will have that much less time and energy to spare for preaching, painting, philosophy, horse-breeding, or whatever his main interest may be. Hence the men with vocations have often betrayed the women who loved them; especially perhaps those whose vocation was for saintliness, who were resolved to put the purity of their souls before everything else. The Buddha deserted his wife and children. Augustine himself lived with a mistress who, he asserts, was very fond of him, and then turned her out with his illegitimate child when he changed his plans; he exhibited remorse for having gone to bed with her, but none for having abandoned her.

'A philosopher ought not to marry,' says John of Salisbury, 'for he cannot at the same time serve wisdom and his wife.' And when one considers how many of the great philosophers were bachelors* one is impressed with the argument. But then one observes that by no means all these bachelors were celibate, and some of them were the fathers of illegitimate children. The sexual urge is admittedly a distraction, and can become obsessive. But obsession with sex is the characteristic frame of mind, not of those who gratify the sexual appetite, but of those who frustrate it; like food, it seems most important when you are short of it. There are indications in the lives of the saints themselves that sexual obsession may be the result of sexual self-denial. Is not the situation with sex like the situation with food and drink? A man is most easily freed from gastronomic distraction if he has someone to supply him regularly with wholesome but not elaborate meals. A man is most easily freed from sexual distraction if he has someone who will supply him with regular satisfaction of his sexual requirements without making too great demands on his devotion: a mistress who will drop in from time to time to go to bed with him, give him a little light conversation and then get out of his way; or better still, a discreet, competent wife who will deal with the petty day-to-day business, keep other distractions at arms' length, and leave him free to pursue his vocation.

But the best wives give far more than sexual relief and efficient housekeeping. If a wife of the wrong sort can be a hindrance to a man with a vocation, a wife of the right sort can be an immense and even an indispensable help to him in achieving the best that is in him. Paul probably made the patriarchal assumption that women are good for nothing but sexual intercourse and household chores; for him there seems to have been no question of a woman contributing to the intellectual, emotional or spiritual development of a man. 'Nothing', said Augustine, quoted with approval by Aquinas, 'so casts down the manly mind from its height as the fondling of a woman.' But if marriage can be a sacrament in the sense of a means to the spiritual

* In addition to the medieval scholastics, these include Plato, Descartes, Hobbes, Locke, Spinoza, Leibniz, Hume and Kant.

growth and fulfilment of the partners, it is not incompatible with the service of God, or with a religious vocation. The rule of clerical celibacy may be justified by the administrative convenience of having officers whose prior devotion is to the corporation and not to their families, men who are free of attachment to localities or the interests of relatives. An order like the Jesuits, holding its men ready to be posted to any part of the world at no notice, may do well to insist on bachelors, for the same reason that the Romans forbade their soldiers to marry. But such a rule deprives them of the enrichment of understanding and sympathy which arises from living in intimacy and love with a person of the other sex. The partnership between man and woman in love and service is among the most valuable things in human experience; it is not easy to show what other things are of greater value. In so far as the mutual giving and receiving of pleasure in the sexual embrace is an expression of love, and an essential element in this partnership, it makes its important contribution to human good. Only misanthropy could condemn it.

We have still to consider the most radical criticism of the puritan view. This is the argument that sexual self-restraint is an intrinsically bad thing, and celibacy reprehensible or crazy. The reason given is that one cannot deny one's sexual appetites without danger to health; perhaps to physical health (a point of view much favoured by men trying to seduce girls), but certainly to health of mind. The principal cause of mental disturbance, it is said, is the frustration of the sexual impulses. If we could get rid of our restrictive customs and see that everybody had plenty of sexual satisfaction, we should all be much healthier and happier. Happiness, according to this doctrine, resides in the satisfaction of a number of fundamental human impulses or instincts, and the persistent frustration of any one of these is certain to lead to unhappiness and unbalance in the personality. If a man does without sex, it is not merely that he loses some enjoyment that he might otherwise have had (as a tone-deaf man has to do without the enjoyment of music). Whereas the enjoyment of music is an incidental thing in human life, and the man who has never had it does not miss it, sex is an essential and universal human want, and the man who has not had it does miss it; the desire is permanently there, pressing for satisfaction. To keep on denying it involves a constant struggle, which diverts mental energies that might be more constructively employed, and wastes and wearies the emotional powers. A man constantly struggling with himself cannot be efficient in his engagements with things and people outside him; he cannot be at peace, he cannot be happy. The trouble he expends in diverting, quietening and appeasing the sexual impulse is that much lost to the healthy pursuit of other satisfactions.

The prevalence of this attitude is largely due to the influence of Freud. So it is worthwhile to see what Freud said and what he did not say on this matter. Freud's problem was to explain how people became neurotic, and his theories were formed in the course of trying to cure those who suffered from obsessive impulses, pointless or exaggerated anxieties, and mysterious attacks of physical pain or weakness with no apparent physical cause. He came to the conclusion that the cause of neurosis always lies in an inner conflict between the conscious self and some unconscious desire, which forces itself into consciousness in a disguised form; the obsessive actions are symbolic fulfilments of repressed desires, the inexplicable physical and mental distress arises when the conscious self acts or tries to act in defiance of some unconscious motive. Dreams, in both normal and neurotic people, provide clues to the character of these repressed desires, since the incidents in dreams, like the obsessive actions of the neurotic, are imaginary fulfilments of unconscious wishes. Freud further held that, when the symbolism is interpreted, the disguises removed (with the help of elaborate and bizarre theories as to the symbolic meaning of dream-happenings), the unconscious desires underlying our dreams and neuroses turn out to be pervasively sexual in character. 'Sexual' is, however, used in a very wide sense: in Freud's writings, not only the act of mating and the stimulation of the genital organs are counted as 'sexual', but also any kind of activity aimed at producing pleasure by means of bodily stimulation, and any sentiment towards another person involving the desire to touch, to be near, or to please the other person; so that, if a child enjoys being stroked or tickled, this counts as a sexual enjoyment, and his liking for his mother's company also comes under the same heading. For Freud thought that all these tendencies spring from the same instinctive sources: the same 'libido' which makes a baby enjoy sucking a dummy and being fondled by its mother develops afterwards into falling in love and mating with an adult of the opposite sex. It is the frustration of this fundamental human instinct which brings about mental illness. It seems easy to draw the inference: neurosis is caused by the frustration of the sexual impulse; let us stop frustrating this impulse and adopt a more permissive sex morality, and we shall be rid of neurosis. But this reasoning is not Freud's, and is not justified by anything that Freud said. It is important to see why not.

In the first place, we must distinguish clearly between inhibiting or controlling an impulse and 'repressing' it. A man who prevents himself from gratifying a strong impulse which he consciously feels need not suffer any psychological damage thereby; the cause of neurosis does not lie in the exercise of deliberate self-control by people who know what they are doing and why. The damage is done when the person is so ashamed and afraid of feeling the impulse that it is expelled from consciousness altogether, so that he ceases to be aware that he has it, and it now operates only in the unconscious: this is the technical meaning of 'repression'. If a soldier in the front line feels afraid of death, knows quite well that he is afraid, takes this as a matter of course and makes no bones about admitting it, then, whether he conquers his fear and goes on fighting or yields to it and runs away, his fear will not make him neurotic. But if he refuses to admit that he is frightened—perhaps because he has been taught that Spartans, or British public-schoolboys, never feel fear, and it is a great disgrace if they do—then the repressed fear goes underground, but does not come to an end, and the man may find himself stricken with paralysis, blindness or dizziness, of which the fear of death, the urge to get out of danger, is the underlying cause.

The habit of repression is formed in childhood; it is a childish, involuntary, irrational way of dealing with desires. In Freudian theory, adult personality is for the most part determined by the experiences of early childhood; and it is then that the essential repressions of sexual desire take place. These repressed desires are primarily incestuous. When a little boy turns his attention from loving himself to loving other people, the first object of his attachment is his mother, and he desires to become her lover, supplanting and even destroying his father (the 'Oedipus complex'). But this desire conflicts with his affection for his father, and with his need to be loved by both parents, and therefore to please and appease them. The conflict leads the child to feel guilty about his incestuous desires and repress them, so that they remain active only in the unconscious. Henceforward, they appear at the conscious level only in a distorted form as dreams and legends, of which the Oedipus legend itself is one. The account of the process in girls is less clear and plausible, but it seems that they have to repress similar attractions towards their fathers.

Such sexual repression takes place in everybody who grows up in a human community. It is an essential part of the process of socialisation; for, as we saw, no human community exists which does not forbid incestuous acts and feelings, and teach its members to regard them as wicked. The repudiation of incestuous sexual desires, which Freud called 'the most maiming wound ever inflicted throughout the ages on the erotic life of man', is a condition of being human. The original and essential taboo is supplemented by other restrictions on the sexual impulses of children, leading to other repressions. These restrictions do damage to human happiness; 'the sexual life of civilised man is seriously disabled'.* But the only way of getting rid of them would be to revert to the level of the brutes. Human society requires the thwarting of sexual impulses, not only, as we have seen, as a condition of cohesion in the family, but also for another reason. The energy of the libido, denied its spontaneous expression in crude sensuality, is transferred or 'sublimated' into substitute satisfactions; and this is the main source of the psychological drive that goes into the intellectual, artistic, religious and commercial activities of civilisation. The beasts have no sexual restraints, and so they have no culture. If we were to abandon the one, we should lose the other. Repression and the liability to neurosis are part of the price we pay for being civilised. Freud thought that modern man pays for his exceptional achievements, his exceptionally high standard of living and of culture, by suffering exceptionally severe restraints on his sexual life and an exceptional liability to neurosis.

But of course, not everybody who passes through this restrictive and repressive training becomes neurotic. Most of us manage to

* Freud, *Civilisation and its Discontents*, Chapter IV.

abandon our sexual designs on our mothers or fathers and transfer our mental energy to socially approved channels while remaining reasonably cheerful and well-balanced, at least while we are awake. If people do become neurotic, Freud held, the explanation is to be found in their early experiences as children. If a person has a sound nervous constitution and is brought up in a sensible way, neither too strictly nor too indulgently, he will be able to adjust himself to the crisis of the Oedipus situation and adapt his libido to the necessary restrictions of social life. It is only if he sets up too sharp a conflict in himself, accumulates too great a load of guilt and too insatiable a conscience, that he is liable to react to the stresses of adult life by developing a neurosis. The emotional relation between child and parent is the decisive factor. Thus what Freud criticises in the main is not the rules of adult sexual behaviour, but the methods of child-training. 'Psychologically, Western European civilisation is fully justified in beginning by censuring any manifestations of the sexual life of children, for there would be no prospect of curbing the sexual desires of adults if the ground had not been prepared for it in child-hood. Nevertheless there is no sort of justification for the lengths beyond this to which civilised society goes in actually denying the existence of these manifestations.'* The danger consists in an attitude in which the strength and pervasiveness of the sexual impulses are not admitted; sex is shrouded in an atmosphere of secrecy, any attempt by a child to understand his physical and emotional development being met with lies, evasion and reproof. What does the damage is not so much the rule that the sexual impulses ought to be controlled as the suggestion that it is wicked to have them at all. The more systematically a child is watched for any sign of sexual interest, which is then immediately reproved, punished or diverted—the more rigorously and carefully, for instance, he is prevented in infancy from handling his genitals, and later in childhood from exploring and interesting himself in the 'facts of life'—the stronger the anger or disapproval which his approaches towards sexual behaviour evoke in those who train him, the greater then will be the risk of harm. Freud's teaching does condemn the practice of telling children that all sexual interests and impulses are evil, for this is most likely to

* Freud, *op. cit.*

cause them to thrust these impulses out of consciousness and pretend to themselves that they do not exist. Freud champions a method of education which is frank and open in its recognition of the sexual, and also the aggressive, elements in childish nature, in the hope of encouraging the child to deal with them himself, not by the repressive method of trying to believe that they are not there, but by the rational adult method of learning to tolerate frustrations and to find alternative and acceptable ways of gratifying desire. While there are many features of Freud's theories which are not generally accepted by psychologists, this one commands wide assent. If we want children to grow up to mental health, we must encourage them to learn how to control their impulses by understanding and accepting them, not by deceiving themselves about them.

Freud's theories are therefore opposed to maintaining the puritan doctrine that sex is intrinsically evil, with its corollary that celibacy is intrinsically superior to marriage. But there is nothing in these theories to lead to the conclusion that sexual abstinence and self-control are necessarily damaging to mental health. If there were, this would be enough to prove the theories false. For it is a matter of plain fact that plenty of celibates are well-balanced people, as free of neurosis as their married neighbours. Priests as a class enjoy a good standard of mental health. Celibacy imposes a strain, of course, just as keeping your temper with naughty children imposes a strain; but both strains are bearable for healthy people, though there may be others more 'highly sexed' or emotionally vulnerable for whom the strain is not bearable without some injury. Again, there is nothing in Freud's doctrines to suggest that an existing neurosis can be cured by sexual gratification. It is clear that once the guilt-complexes have been established in childhood, a neurotic who fulfils his sexual desires in defiance of deep-seated emotional repugnances may make his inner conflicts worse and not better.

4

The Romantic Attitude

At the present day much thinking on sexual morality is dominated by romantic ideas of the subject. Defining the term 'romantic' is a difficult task. Dozens of definitions have been produced,* especially in the fields of literature and music, and there seems to be no good reason for preferring any one of them. We therefore give our own definition of romanticism as the view that moral rules and social institutions, like artistic forms, may all be disregarded in the interest of undergoing or expressing intense personal experience enhanced by the powers of imagination. Art and sex are the main fields of expression for the romantic tendency. We might be tempted to dismiss the romantic person as an unthinking egoist who merely seeks the big thrill, but we should be wrong; he is a man with a vision. He aims at flooding the entire outer world with the inward radiance of his own imagination. The weakness of his position is that where facts fail to coincide with his dream, he will not take them seriously.

Now let us see what romantics make of sexual morality. They hold that the love relationship between man and woman is the most important of all human ties, in that it gives rise to the only sort of emotional ecstasy of which ordinary people are capable. Mystical experience is said to be the peak of human bliss, but it lies within the scope of so very few. The romantic treats sexual love as though it were the common man's mystical experience. To anyone who takes this view, rules of premarital chastity or marital fidelity may at first

* These are listed in J. Barzun, *Classical, Romantic and Modern*, Chapter X: 'Romantic: a sampling of modern usage'.

appear unimportant as compared with the individual's aspirations towards his supreme moment of experience. His highest destiny is to be self-transcendent through sexual union with another. Beside this, nothing else in life can count for much. The moment of self-transcendence not only beckons him on, like the princes in fairy-tales, through every sort of difficulty and danger; once attained, he sees it as justifying everything else in his life. It fulfils him. It raises him to a higher power. In its way it is an experience of conversion. His love becomes a sun whose light irradiates whatever he sees, conferring value on things that others would find commonplace. Let them scoff: he has the conviction of his ecstasy!

Some people are so unfortunate as never to fall in love. Others do it repeatedly, raising the question whether the supreme experience of love can really be, as is sometimes claimed, a unique happening, once for all time, with a partner often thought of as the predestined choice. And does it still count if one's delight in The Other is unreciprocated? Can the genuine romantic find his greatest joy in a one-sided relationship? It takes a sophisticate, someone very tough-minded, to accept that love's delight may be a solitary flight of the imagination, unshared by its object but none the less life-justifying. Characteristic romantic love-experiences are the throb of passion, the shaft in the heart, the shudder of delight. Whatever the price to be paid for them, they are held worthy of it, tokens of a world within of intense and vivid feeling for which money, fame or even daily sufficiency are well lost, moral rules exist only to be broken and social institutions to be disregarded. Unromantic readers may find it hard to accept that what we have been describing is actually the experience of many, but it is so. Some after a while forget. For others it remains the core of life. In either case it is psychologically unrealistic to deride or ignore it.

Everyone who falls in love in this way is a romantic, even if only for a little while. He is living intensely through the transforming power of his imagination. The difference between pure animal lust and ecstatic love is just this arousing in ecstatic love of dormant imaginative power. Once it has been aroused, the imagination may never again become entirely quiescent, and love may permanently give emotional colouring to life.

In his romantic phase everyone believes the world well lost for love. Nevertheless, if he has the choice, his preference is for the enduring relationship of marriage rather than the isolated love-affair, which so often dies of satiety because the loving pair have no common enterprise beyond their love. They spend, as it were, a holiday together; they never function as a working partnership with a home to put together and tend, a family to produce and rear, a job to be done together year in year out. Their relationship.can easily be too far out on a limb. Of course, this generalisation is not intended to apply to all extra-marital love affairs, since some are overtures to marriage, others indispensable supplements or props to married life. But the romantic wants above all things to be happily married. And marriage, he feels, should be based on mutual love and trust, an absolutely comprehensive relationship in which each gives his all, and man and wife are equal partners. Nothing less. So by true romantics marriage will always be preferred to extra-marital relationships because only marriage can give full assurance that both partners intend it to last happily ever after; only marriage (or relationships that are marriage in everything but name) can provide the range of occupations shared, the freedom to be together at all times and in all places that a man and a woman need if they are to develop all the potentialities of their feeling for each other. Love affairs outside marriage are almost always lop-sided, over-weighted with passion and mutual possessiveness. After the first few encounters there is so often the feeling that if you do not go to bed together whenever the opportunity arises you are letting slip the irretrievable, and so you do it even without any passionate desire. On the other hand, circumstances often lead to frustration which by itself can spoil a promising relationship. Then, too, the knowledge that the affair might soon come to a close makes many lovers unwilling to invest in it as much patience and consideration as they might bring to married life. On all these grounds the thoughtful romantic moralist will take successful marriage to be the goal of his endeavours and regard premarital affairs as at best preliminary try-outs where useful knowledge may be gained of one's own and one's partner's needs and propensities. On the other hand, the adulterous affair may be the logical concomitant of a mistaken marriage. Promiscuity is something for which the romantic has no use. How could anyone have the intensest of all possible feelings for someone who just happened to turn up when he was in the mood? The romantic in love gives his all, and demands all in return. If all is to be exchanged for all, clearly marriage is the logical outcome. Admittedly, those novelists and poets who are the chief exponents of the romantic view tend to deal mainly in cases of thwarted passion, but this is because the story of a love match without complications could be rather dull, unless narrated with surpassing skill. Hence the fevered tone peculiar to romantic tales, in which fantastic complexities abound. Fortunately, in life itself feeling cannot long be sustained at this pitch. The lovers marry and get used to their felicity, the astonishing harmony of their natures becomes a matter of course, and they settle down to the weaving of the marriage relationship, a task that husbands and wives neglect at their peril. This day-by-day fitting together of habits and inclinations, with uncounted mutual concessions and disappointments, occasional boredom, but unexpected bonuses and revelations, this interlacing of two individuals to make a pair, is miraculous and indescribable, even by romantic writers.

In the characteristic romantic doctrine of marriage, the partners have equal emotional rights. This presupposes that the woman is held in high esteem, and is not merely the idealised instrument of masculine passion. Each partner aims at becoming more nearly complete. So the husband must develop his feminine tendencies, the wife her masculine ones. As Keyserling put it, marriage is a magnetic field of attraction between the male and female poles, with mutual interchange of particles. As instances we might quote the free and daring, almost manly attitudes of Goethe's two Charlottes in *The Elective Affinities* and *The Sorrows of Young Werther*, and the dreamy feminine emotionalising of his heroes, men who instead of trying to live with their problems, resort to flight, Werther to suicide and Edward to the wars.

These two novels of Goethe's (1774 and 1809) stand at the fountain-head of the romantic tradition in literature. The romantic love story does indeed go back at least as far as the second century A.D. with *Daphnis and Chloe*, which reads rather like the scenario of an early Hollywood film. And a great deal of medieval fiction is on the theme of knightly devotion to ladies; but the ladies were usually married to someone else and the knights made other arrangements for the satisfaction of their sexual urges. Medieval romantic attachment was depicted as an emotional experience transcending bodily appetite and quite unconnected with the institution of marriage or the raising of children, matters arranged by heads of families for reasons of wealth and power. We do not meet with romanticism proper until the unworldly devotion of the medieval knights becomes linked with physical union and sexual fidelity to form an ideal of marriage replacing family interests in lands and influence as the principle of marital selection.

In Goethe's two novels we find poignant outcries of thwarted love from the heroes who cannot hope to marry the objects of their adoration, Werther because she has unfeelingly married another man, Edward because it is he himself who is already married. No matter: they still dwell on the impossible union. Edward says: 'No, I never loved before. It is only now that I know what life means. Till now what I had called life was nothing but its prelude . . . amusement, sport to kill time with. I never lived till I knew her, till I loved her entirely and only her. . . . I should like to see the man who outdoes me in the talent of love. A miserable life it is, full of anguish and tears, but it is so natural, so dear to me, that I could hardly change it for another.' And Werther: 'I cannot understand how she can love another, how she dares love another when I love nothing in this world so completely, so devotedly as her, when I know only her and have no other possession than her in the world.' Werther and his imitators had a tremendous vogue in the drawing-rooms of the early nineteenth century, so much so that one wonders whether without them Keats would ever have dared express himself as he does in this letter dated May 1820, even though he was at the time consumptive and emotionally overcharged:

MY DEAREST GIRL,

I wrote a Letter for you yesterday expecting to have seen your mother. I shall be selfish enough to send it though I know it may give you a little pain, because I wish you to see how unhappy I am for love of you, and endeavour as much as I can to entice you to give up your whole heart to me whose whole existence hangs upon you. You could not step or move an eyelid but it would shoot to my heart—I am greedy of you. Do not think of anything but me. . . . Well may you exclaim, how selfish, how cruel, not to let me enjoy my youth! To wish me to be unhappy! You must be so if you love me—upon my Soul I can be contented with nothing else. If you could really what is called enjoy yourself at a party—if you can smile in people's faces, and wish them to admire you *now* you never have nor ever will love me. . . . If we love we must not live as other men and women do— I cannot brook the wolfsbane of fashion and foppery and tattle. You must be mine to die upon the rack if I want you. . . .

And again, in a letter of 25 July 1819: 'I have two luxuries to brood over in my walks, your Loveliness and the hour of my death. Oh that I could have possession of them both in the same minute!' At an earlier date the emotional tone of Goethe's lovers and of Keats would hardly have been considered manly.

And here is Shelley, expressing the general principle of the romantic conception of love, in similar vein: 'The discovery of its antitype: the meeting with an understanding capable of clearly estimating our own; an imagination which should enter into and seize upon the subtle and delicate peculiarities which we have delighted to cherish and unfold in secret, with a frame whose nerves, like the chords of two exquisite lyres strung to the accompaniment of one delightful voice, vibrate with the vibrations of our own; and a combination of all these in such proportions as the type within demands; this is the invisible and unattainable point to which love tends, and to attain which it urges forth the powers of man to arrest the faintest shadow of that, without the possession of which there is no rest or respite to the heart over which it rules' (*On Love*). That this view of love gained wide currency is shown by Jane Austen's guying of it in the character of Marianne in *Sense and Sensibility*. Marianne, however, grew to know better and be happy to marry a humdrum fellow who prosaically protected his health with a flannel waistcoat, whereas Shelley and other writers preaching the romantic gospel of union between emotional equals (Schleiermacher, Schlegel, Tieck and A. E. Hoffmann) experienced sad disappointments in their love affairs and marriages. Too much may be asked from the outset by the thoroughgoing romantic, too much emotional intensity, too lively a response, and correspondingly too little common sense.

The romantic ideal of love was carried into the drawing-rooms of the period by yet another medium, the *Lied* or song setting of a lyric, including several by Goethe himself, by Heine, Schiller, Müller, Eichendorff, Rückert and Chamisso. Many of these lyrics are still well known today because of their exquisite settings by Schubert and Schumann. They are perhaps the most characteristic expression of romanticism, celebrating the poet's reactions to landscape, seasonal change, sunset, moonlight and the grimness of winter as well as his joys and sufferings in the throes of love. Nowadays we often find it less embarrassing to conceal the more exaggerated sentiments of these verses by singing them in the original German. A comparison between these and the lyrics set by the Elizabethans is instructive. Whereas the Elizabethan poet praises his lady's lips and breasts, and outspokenly reproaches her for not admitting him to her bed, the romantic poet seems never to think of crossing the threshold of her house, but pours out his longing in some of the world's most delightful music, aspiring at most to a kiss, content to devote his days and nights to brooding over discarded ribbons and withered posies.

The romantic poets, novelists and composers found imitators at more popular levels, so that the nineteenth century saw a proliferation of drawing-room ballads, album leaves and novelettes, in which the original intensity of romantic feeling was watered down and vulgarised into characteristic Victorian sentimentality, persisting in lower-middle-class parlours until the end of the First World War. The popular drawing-room ballads, and more recently jazz lyrics, as well as romantic novelettes, show an exclusive concentration on amorous emotion which is quite untempered by irony and strikes more critical audiences as ridiculous. And there can be no doubt that these popular items have played a part in moulding the ideas of young girls about sexual love and morality. Hence the notion that excess in love is something admirable, to which all other things should give way, is a common one, confirmed by all the voices of popular entertainment. At the same time intensive industrialisation has made romantic escapism more seductive than ever before. Young people tend to fall in love with love. Here, they feel, is an experience to which every one of them has a right. If it cannot be honestly come by, then it has to be 'dreamed up'. Romantic ideas of love have also accentuated the mutual possessiveness of lovers to the point at which it is now considered reasonable to begin 'going steady' in the early 'teens, and married pairs take it for granted that their social life shall be conducted as an indivisible combine, sacrificing any friends and interests that they do not happen to share.

We may fruitfully contrast this idea of marriage with that still common in Italy, where the married pair continue to form part of the extended family or clan, and are obliged to put its interests before their wishes as a couple. 'The Italian family', says Barzini, 'is a stronghold in a hostile land; within its walls and among its members the individual finds consolation, help, advice, provisions, loans, weapons, allies and accomplices to aid him in his pursuits. No Italian who has a family is ever alone. . . . No Italian can lightly abandon the wife who is the mother of his first-born male child. . . . The family must be deferred to, enriched, made powerful, respected and feared, by the use of whatever means are necessary. . . . Its honour must not be tarnished. All wrongs done to it must be avenged. Every member is duty bound, when it is inevitable, to sacrifice his life. Men have spent their last penny to save a relative from bankruptcy. . . . Marriages are naturally important, as decisive for the promotion of the influence and prosperity of an ordinary family as they were in royal families of old. Many sons and daughters of prominent political leaders are married to each other, hostages in each other's camps'. . . . 'The Italian male, the head or heir of the family, is justly famous the world over for his manliness. He jealously defends his independence. No woman submits him to her will.' These statements frame the very antithesis of romantic marriage between two individuals who, together with their children, constitute a little world of their own, isolated as far as may be from all other persons.

The persistence of romantic ideas of love and marriage is still so marked in present-day Britain and North America that no normally reared English-speaking boy or girl could begin to understand marriage as it is in Italy. And the characteristic romantic inflation of emotional expectations is a permanent cause of unhappiness in

English and American life. How did it become so deeply rooted in the English scene?

One possible cause immediately presents itself—there are doubtless others, but the one we shall discuss is the reaction against the effects of industrialisation. Both Britain and the U.S.A. were involved in the industrial revolution much earlier and to a greater extent than Italy, where romantic ideas of love and marriage have been taken far less seriously. English-speaking men and women of all classes from the early years of the nineteenth century onwards have felt, however remotely, the pressure of the machine age on their personal lives. To those living in industrial areas the blight of air pollution and the presence of humming machinery on the doorstep, down the street or in the air, have been constant reminders of how small an area is left for the private life of pleasing oneself. The machine is a tireless master, often an ugly, dirty and noisy neighbour. To those living near motorways or airports even the motor engine has come to seem a doubtful blessing. But in the earlier years of the industrial revolution, dirt and noise were even more obtrusive, and as a result many inhabitants of industrial areas fled from them into the recesses of their own imaginations. They began to read novelettes—those who could not read used to be read to—and the Sunday papers began to supplement the novelettes with amazing stories of actual events. The world of romantic reverie nourished by mass entertainment came into being to make life endurable to the victims of industrialisation, and perhaps, too, for dwellers in dull little towns and the increasingly depopulated countryside, two types of environment from which the industrial revolution was gradually sucking the vitality. In their day-dreams people escape to a world more nearly fashioned after the heart's desire, where they can be themselves untrammelled and glorious, intoxicated with other untrammelled and glorious people, romantically in love. This is one of the great refuges of the harassed individual in a highly mechanised society. It is equally his refuge against bureaucracy, large-scale organisations, hydrogen bombs and the concrete jungle. It is not for everyone that romantic love is the refuge; some find it in rock-climbing, some in sailing little boats, others in identifying with heroes of startling adventures in print or on the screen. But for women most of the time, and for many men when they are at the mating stage, romantic love is a private oasis in the desert of industrial society.

The really basic romantic idea of marriage is that people ought to marry because they are in love rather than for any other reason. Ideally, the young couple should fall in love with each other almost simultaneously, and for both it should be the first time. Neither will feel any doubts. Whatever the obstacles, they should resolutely win through to the altar, and onward to perfect felicity in a shared home which neither cares to leave without the other. It follows that social life, friends, leisure activities and holidays must all be in common. The absolute mutual loyalty of the pair must not be marred by a single straying thought. The foundation of this mutual regard is the marriage bed. Quarrels will always be followed by the sweetest of reconciliations. Children will be desired and welcomed as the fulfilment of physical union; when they grow up and go away to make homes of their own, the happy parents will enjoy a second honeymoon. Intercourse will continue with unabated enthusiasm into a ripe old age. This is the picture of married life given by Marie Stopes in *Married Love* and *Enduring Passion*, published in 1918 and 1928 respectively, and destined to become standard handbooks on the ideal, the techniques and the morality of married life for at least two generations. It is also the ideal pattern held up by the Marriage Guidance Council for young people to bear in mind, and something very like it forms the ideal Christian marriage of our own society. In this sort of married life differences of opinion are amicably resolved. Neither partner exploits the other. Joys and sorrows, like pocket-money, are shared. Each takes the lead where he or she is the better qualified to do so. Jealousy there is none, because no ground for it is given. On every matter of importance the two act as one, setting their children that example of marital harmony which is the best training they can have for happy marriages of their own. It is a beautiful ideal, which some couples do realise, and marriage on this pattern is beyond doubt the best of human relationships.

What criticisms then can be made of the romantic ideal? Mainly this: that the standard set is so high, the expectations aroused so inflated, that few elderly married couples could honestly claim that they have always lived even near to the requisite level of virtue and bliss. In the close and continuous contact of marriage it is rarely possible to ignore facts of character and situation which fail to coincide with romantic dreams of one's partner. Against his will the married romantic sees the disparities and, because he has tended to expect so much, may feel disillusioned. This is one of the rocks on which marriages can break up. Like any other deliberate search for happiness, marriage that is too self-consciously oriented on romantic lines is likely to prove disappointing. Perhaps the first principle of married life is not to expect too much of each other. Maybe the trouble is that in marriage romantics seek access to an ecstatic type of experience that is not to be obtained by self-assertion, but only through a letting-slip of one's individuality. If this is so, the romantic often spoils his own chances of happiness through his characteristic emphasis on his own individuality and his expectation that in marriage it will be enhanced.

In a world constructed to fit romantic attitudes, there would be a Miss Right for every young man, and vice versa. Everyone would fall in love once only, and for life. The problem would be simply how to discover one's 'elective affinity' among the circle of eligible young people, and all difficulties would end, as Victorian novels commonly ended, with the wedding. Alas, we do not live in this kind of world! Just as some people never get the measles, others never fall in love in the standard romantic manner. Perhaps the full flavour of the experience has never been enjoyed (if 'enjoyed' is the right word) by more than a minority of people. Whether a youngster falls romantically in love or not partly depends on whether he has the right kind of temperament. It also depends on whether romantic love is the expected thing in his social group. Just as in some religious communities a young person is expected to have an emotional experience of religious conversion at a certain age, and a high proportion of young people do have such an experience of greater or lesser intensity, whereas in other communities which have no such tradition this rarely happens, so it is with falling in love. There are susceptible folk who will do it whatever the circumstances, and others who are constitutionally immune, although they may be capable of a loyal and affectionate relationship in marriage; and there are many more who will fall in love more intensely or less intensely according to the fashion of the society in which they live. One commonly falls in love because one is ripe and ready for it, and on the look-out for someone to fall in love with. There is a large element of suggestion in the experience. The lover has, even if subconsciously, a preconceived notion of what he is looking for, and his desire to be in love predisposes him to see the wished-for qualities in some girl he meets, whether or not they really are present. It is evident that what Dante saw in Beatrice was largely the product of his own imagination, and independent of the actual personality of Beatrice, whom after all he hardly knew. We may infer that Beatrice could have been replaced by a girl with a different personality without this making much difference to Dante's romantic image (which he took care not to spoil, for he kept his distance and married somebody else). But if a man actually marries some young woman whose features he has unwittingly superimposed on the picture in his own imagination, he is due for disappointment, not to say outrage, when he discovers the difference between the picture and the reality. As a romantic, Dante knew best.

Again, if *A* falls romantically in love with *B*, there is no guarantee in real life that *B* will reciprocate. (How different from the world of the 'elective affinities'!) It is true that his being in love with her will enhance his attractiveness in her eyes; it is unusual not to feel flattered at being thus singled out. And he will naturally put himself in the most favourable light. If she also is in a susceptible condition, this may be enough. But there are contra-suggestible types who are only attracted by those who are indifferent to them or downright hostile; for these love is a blood-sport which must partake of the excitement, uncertainty and danger of the chase. It is difficult for such people to contract romantically satisfactory marriages.

To complicate matters further, romantic passion is commonly a temporary condition. A couple who have been married for years may still love each other, but the thrill is not the same; romance has developed insidiously into a different sort of love relationship, which has, however, a better chance of lasting. The unlucky people are those whose romantic feelings have evaporated and all that remains is indifference or even dislike. Dislike is more likely if the original thrill was founded on illusions.

It seems that romantic love is no sufficient basis for married happiness. It brings people together, it gives them the enthusiasm to embark on a partnership; but it is not a magic elixir for happy married life. 'Love is all, love is all' may be a beguiling line for a song, but it is not a sound recipe for wedlock. Of course, there are various recipes. Most of the successful ones call for the ingredients of shared enjoyment of activities outside bed; of complementary matching of abilities, so that the pair as a pair has as few shortcomings as possible; of temperamental fit, such as the lively with the phlegmatic; of considerable patience and mutual forbearance; of goodwill and the steady resolution that this marriage is going to last as something over and above its constituent personalities. A marriage which has been steadily built up over a number of years is an entity to be reckoned with, and its partners really have something to lose by separation, whatever the temptations of a new love. Whereas compatibility and forbearance without the help of romance may produce a good enough marriage, romance without compatibility and forbearance will certainly make a bad one. The mischief of the romantic theory is that it may lead young people to imagine that a marital relation is possible without disappointments, conflicts, boredom and even moments of white-hot hatred. When the romantic encounters these, having been led to expect perfection, he loses heart and supposes his marriage a failure. He wanted mutual intoxication that would last indefinitely; when it fades from his marriage, there is a risk that he will seek it elsewhere. This is exactly what happened to such champions of romantic love as Shelley and Bertrand Russell. The new love will always have some attractions that were lacking in the old one, and because it *is* new and untried it tends to weigh more heavily in the scale. Quite irrationally it is expected to retain that enchantment which the old has already lost. Sometimes it is the children of the marriage whose interests prevent a break-up, especially if it is the wife who is being tempted. But the romantic view of love does encourage people to feel that the individual's right to intense experience has priority over everything else.

This is where the romantic view of sexual morality does the greatest damage of which it is capable. Nothing in the field of sexual relationships could be worse than the break-up of a marriage in good working order simply because husband or wife has romantic expectations of intenser experience with someone else. Existing difficulties in the marriage (of which there are always a few) are pressed into service as reasons for ending it; what could perfectly well be lived with before the new opportunity came on the scene is suddenly found intolerable and a fit excuse for divorce. But in a system of sexual morality in which marriage is indissoluble, although there may be no shortage of temptations to infidelity, the marriage itself oftener persists as a genuine marriage, sometimes winning through to a new and more satisfying equilibrium.

Romantic sex morality always seems to exact great tolerance from the spouse who is on the verge of being discarded. It is not a question of a temporary joyride for the other, but of his/her sacred right to permanent maximum intensity of experience, which he/she clearly is not getting out of the present relationship. There are always those who will suggest that the discarded partner is the one who is most to blame, and so must be obliged to let the other go free. Is he/she still deeply in love with the unfaithful one? Whose is the intense experience which matters more? Two count for more than one, so the adulterous couple on this principle must get their way, unless indeed the effect on the children is given priority, as sometimes happens.

Waning mutual interest sometimes brings about marriages in which husband and wife both feel themselves perfectly free to have additional love affairs; these have long been a feature of 'advanced' circles. A well-known example was the second marriage of Bertrand Russell, who lived up to his own stated conviction: 'I shall not teach that faithfulness to our partner through life is any way desirable, or that a permanent marriage should be regarded as excluding temporary episodes.'* One has the impression that such marriages are commoner in middle-class families now that more wives go out to work, meeting other men, driving their own cars which give them some privacy for love-making, and having less time and interest to spare for their husbands, who retaliate with love-affairs of their own. Lack of opportunity always has been one of the most important bars to any attempt to realise romantic ideas of a marriage better than this one; the working wife both has and gives to her husband increased opportunities. In this type of situation however the romantic ideal of love easily degenerates into matter-of-fact sensualism.

* *Education and the Good Life.*

A tendency now showing itself is to put marriage on a competitive basis, so that each partner has to 'hold' the other against all rivals. The wronged wife is then seen as a failure, and the Other Woman as a success; if the wife will not divorce, the Other Woman becomes a stock romantic heroine. She used to be a kept woman, but nowadays she will have a job of her own; the doting adulterous husband merely provides her with supplementary luxuries.

Romantic sex morality gives rise to a nexus of physical rights and duties within marriage different from those of patriarchal morality. Husband and wife being emotionally equal, it becomes the duty of the husband to pay attention to the desires and needs of his wife, not to force himself on her sexually when she is tired or simply unwilling, not to attempt penetration before she is fully stimulated, and, if he is able, to prolong intercourse until she is satisfied. In the first respect, most savage codes, and the ancient Jewish code we quoted earlier, display more concern than modern ones, for they usually specify periods such as those of menstruation, pregnancy and lactation when intercourse is forbidden. But the duties of adequate stimulation and satisfaction are recognised by neither the patriarchal nor the puritan code, and it is only gradually that these implications of the romantic code are being recognised. Similarly, we are coming to think of it as wrong for a woman to use a man merely as a means to provide her with children, without caring for him personally or taking any interest in his sexual delight. According to puritan morality her attitude would be highly moral, but according to romantic morality it is selfish and callous.

Of course, even in the most favourable circumstances, some will marry those whom they neither love nor respect, for money, position, security, to get away from home, or so as not to be outdone by their contemporaries in the marital rat-race. It is absurd to expect every match to be a love match, and doubtful whether the net rate of marital happiness would go up if every match were. But there is something wrong when either partner enters the alliance with the intention of getting as much and giving as little as possible. And this can happen in passionate as well as in calculating matches. An individual loves as he is: if he is selfish, grasping, pretentious and over-bearing in other contexts, he will love in this fashion too, however passionately, and his objective in loving will be to possess and to subjugate; consciously or unconsciously, he is out to exploit, and the strict romantic moralist will find him outrageous.

In view of the exacting marital requirements of romantic morality, it is the more important in a society dominated by it that young people should be given both adequate sexual education and plenty of opportunity for meeting a wide range of possible life partners. Adequate sexual education does not stop short at an outline of the physiology of reproduction; it goes on to describe the emotional background of the stages of courtship and mating, stressing the differences of response and outlook between boy and girl and discussing the problems that can arise out of these. It is not reasonable to leave young people to grope their way into the most important personal relationship of their lives. Shortsighted, love may be; we do wrong to blindfold it altogether.

In England, where the majority of schools for those aged 11 and over segregate girls from boys, only the small percentage who go on to technical college or university have opportunities for discovering possible mates in the class or lecture room. In America co-education and more widespread church and chapel attendance seem to provide altogether more extensive opportunities for social contacts between the sexes. In small towns, like Elmtown of August B. Hollingshead's *Elmtown's Youth* (1949), and in the one-class suburban developments mentioned by Vance Packard in Chapter 6 of *The Status Seekers* (pp. 88 *et seq.*), rigid class stratification together with more community activity than is usual in England, brings together groups of boys and girls who would be considered socially eligible marriage partners. But when I was studying the social life of Henley-in-Arden, in England in the late 1940s[*], I found no such pattern of picnics, hayrides, large-scale parties or even club activities for young people, as even the Youth Club was not a success. In England it is still possible for boy or girl to have to rely on finding someone suitable from among the sisters or brothers of friends, the friends of brothers or sisters, the immediate neighbours, or someone met at work. But it is possible to be an only child, with friends whose brothers or sisters are in the wrong age groups, working apart from contemporaries of the

---

[*] *Littletown in Overspill*, by W. M. Whiteley, in *Living in Towns*, ed. L. Kuper, Cresset Press, 1953.

opposite sex, living in a block where there are few or none of them, and not belonging to a church. This situation is not so common as it was in the 1930s when both of us were in it, and moreover had friends of our own sex similarly situated, some of whom have never married. And at the present day we still hear of our friends' children from single-sex schools marrying the first comer, apparently because they believe there will be no more. The gang habit provides some with a choice of partners at the appropriate social level, but it seems unlikely that the dance halls and café bars where most gangs meet are satisfactory *milieux* in which to observe and choose a possible mate. (We understand that in our suburb an all-night launderette is the new convenient rendezvous for youngsters on the look-out for one another.) Small wonder that 'Get yours now' is the maxim that guides some teenagers in their courting days! But they should be meeting in attractive premises where the prime interest is in things to do and to enjoy, and pairing-off takes place gradually and naturally between those who find themselves brought together through a common interest. The average English youth club, starved of funds and offering little more than dancing, pop records, table tennis and sometimes a drama group, is a faint shadow of what it could be if, instead of expecting to be subsidised in their leisure occupations, the young people could be persuaded to pay the club dues which nowadays most of them can well afford. They could then have a wide range of craft and sport activities in a club atmosphere far removed from the chilly aura of our evening institutes. This is one way of widening the marital choice for some at least of our young people to include others of their own kind—a better prospect for married life than the ordinary love affair between two who have nothing in common save love and children. As companionship, watching side by side the same television programme is a poor substitute for both belonging to the same lively drama group, playing duets, gardening or both participating in some indoor or outdoor game. Once a couple have drifted into the position where the husband goes to the pub and the wife to the Bingo hall several times a week they have squandered their chance of happy companionship. In England we do not take seriously enough either the provision of opportunities for young people to meet, or the establishment of common interests.

At the other extreme we have the American custom of early and competitive dating between co-educated teenagers. Here there is no problem about meeting possible partners. The trouble is that they begin far too young, when petting is unlikely to be anything more than a game, but still rather a dangerous one, since it throws together unchaperoned children whose curiosity and desire to keep up with their contemporaries may well involve them in advanced love-making before they are emotionally ready for it. This can hardly be a sound apprenticeship in sexual matters. Love-making is or should be more than a game between precocious children. It is difficult to find out how much distortion of emotional development results from beginning to court so early in life, in the competitive atmosphere in which girls are feted as 'The Most Dated Girl of her College Year', and so on. What has this sort of caper to do with the search for a suitable spouse? It seems a waste of the built-in advantages of the American system of throwing both sexes together from the start. One wonders whether this premature initiation into courtship rituals before they can mean much to the participants does not in many cases produce an emotional blockage that is never overcome; hence unsatisfactory marriages between individuals who have remained immature.

Both countries need a more realistic approach to courtship, treating it as a preparation for married life with a settled habit of husband and wife doing side by side as many different things as they can.

To sum up the themes of this chapter. The romantic person values, beyond any rule or institution, feelings that have been abnormally intensified by imagination. It follows that he does not care for promiscuity because it leaves no room for extremes of emotion. His sexual goal is successful marriage, which he sees as affording the best opportunities for the life of unstinted feeling between two people in love. To him premarital love affairs are only training gallops, although adultery may be justifiable when a marriage has failed. His expectations from marriage are unduly high, taking into account the failings of most of us. Probably if less were expected and more given in the marriage relationship, there would be more highly satisfactory marriages. So the romantic ideal, beautiful as it is, endangers marriages in that people who expect to realise it and fail to do so tend to fling away what they *have* achieved in wedlock for the sake of starting all over again, often with no better outcome. Romantic sex morality also puts pressure on the rejected spouse to concede his partner's right to a new love, superseding what is claimed to have been a failure. But adultery need not lead to divorce. Among realistic people it may function as a prop to the marriage! The overall tendency of the romantic moralist is utilitarian: that is, he believes that the criterion of a good relationship is the amount of happiness it yields—the better the relationship, the greater the happiness. Marriage, he holds, should be based on love, without regard for other factors. Unfortunately he tends to set an unrealistically high standard of continuous mutual appreciation between the couple. If the romantic ideal is to be a useful guide, it must be modified by realistic considerations—people must agree not to expect the impossible either of one another or of themselves.

5

Unfruitful Sex

Our concern so far has been almost entirely with 'normal' mating: that is, the stimulation of each other's genitals by man and woman leading to the penetration of the woman by the man, followed by his emission of semen. Only this kind of sexual activity is capable of begetting children. But it is by no means the only form of sexual activity that is capable of giving pleasure, easing tension, or arousing and expressing love. The kinds of sexual stimulation which are not capable of producing children are commonly called 'perversions'. The name implies condemnation: it suggests that these activities are not only different from normal mating, but worse. This is in fact the attitude of the European moral tradition. We shall be using the word 'perversion' merely as a description without any moral implications.

There are a great variety of perversions. There is mating with non-human animals—'bestiality'. There is stimulation of his (her) own genitals by the individual, by hand or whatever other means are found convenient—'masturbation'. There is stimulation of the genitals of a man or boy by another male or of a woman by another woman—'homosexuality', or in the female case 'lesbianism', of which there are various forms (between males, 'buggery' or 'sodomy', the penetration of the back passage, is much less common than mutual masturbation). In intercourse between man and woman, there is also the stimulation of the genitals with the hand or the mouth, whether in addition to or as a substitute for penetration. (There are even those who regard as a perversion intercourse taking place in any position except when the man is lying over the woman.) And there is normal mating in which by some means or other conception is prevented from taking place. There are many ways of doing this: by the man withdrawing before emission ('coitus interruptus'), by interposing a sheath worn by the man or a cap worn by the woman between the semen and the mouth of the womb, by the use of chemicals which destroy the sperm or prevent the deposition of ova, by confining intercourse to a period in which the woman is infertile, or by surgical operations rendering either party sterile.

Moral systems differ in their attitude to perversions. Some primitive societies are easy-going about them, seeing no particular harm in them. The ancient Greeks tolerated male homosexuality, and the Hindu *Kama Sutra* gives detailed instructions about how to enjoy it. But most civilised codes have condemned some, if not all, perversions. The Hebrew code from which we quoted fiercely denounces bestiality and male homosexuality. This condemnation presents in a particularly acute form the difficulties we noticed at the beginning of this book. On the face of it, there is no *harm* in any of these performances. In so far as they give pleasure, there is some good in them. Nor can those who denounce them often give any coherent reason for their hostility. At the same time, this hostility is often felt with great vehemence and passion. Sodomy is 'the abominable crime', 'the crime against nature' —'*the* abominable crime', as though there were something about it which made it particularly loathsome by comparison with embezzlement, perjury, malicious wounding or, for that matter, rape. What is there about it? When one finds a thinker of the eminence of St Thomas Aquinas firmly laying it down that masturbation is a graver sin than rape,* one wonders what process of thought or feeling can have led him to a view so inhumane.

We have not here to deal with an instinctive repulsion. All these perversions are common; all of them attract some people, and some attract very large numbers of people. Kinsey's investigation of a very large sample of Americans found that 93 per cent of males and 62 per cent of females† had indulged in masturbation, about 50 per cent of males and 28 per cent of females had had some homosexual experience, and even bestiality was admitted by 8 per cent of males

---

* *Summa Theologiae*, II, ii, 154.
† Earlier investigations yielded figures of over 70 per cent for females.

and $3\frac{1}{2}$ per cent of females. The disgust people feel about these practices is clearly not inborn. (To a normal heterosexual male, buggery
may indeed seem filthy; but this is quite insufficient to account for the
fervour with which homosexuality is denounced. There are quite a
lot of people, not all of them female, to whom all sexual relations
seem filthy; this also is a learned, not an innate attitude.) The warmth
of the hostility towards perversions is not easy to account for. Perhaps
those who feel it most strongly are fighting against repressed tendencies of the same kind in themselves. Perhaps the sexual emotions
we have all learned to hold in check burst out violently whenever
our aggression is licensed by public opinion. Whatever the explanation,
we shall assume that feelings of abhorrence against perversions, which
are felt very strongly by some people but not at all by others, are in
themselves no reason for condemning these practices. We are justified in condemning only if we can find other and solider reasons.

There is in fact one system of ideas which gives a thorough and
reasoned explanation of what is wrong with perversions. And as it
covers all of them at once, and also influences the thought of many
people today, we must examine it carefully. This is the theory of
'natural' behaviour, based on ideas of Aristotle and still part of the
dominant philosophy of Catholicism. According to this line of thought,
what is wrong with perversions is that they are 'unnatural' or 'against
nature'. What this means is by no means obvious. Calling them 'unnatural' does not mean that they do not 'come naturally' to people;
we have seen that they do. Nor does 'unnatural' mean 'uncommon'
or 'unusual'; for at least one of the perversions, masturbation, is
normal in the sense that most people do it. And even if a practice is
rare, this is no reason against it; so are left-handedness, teetotalism and
a liking for the music of Bach. There is no virtue in being like most
other people, and Aristotle and his followers never thought there was.
It is said that what is 'unnatural' is 'against the intention of nature'.
But this is puzzling. Nature could have intentions only if 'Nature'
was the name of a person. But there is no such person as Nature, and
therefore no such intentions as Nature's intentions. Thunderstorms
are natural phenomena, and usually damaging to men, but they are
not *intended* to do us harm. And if there were such a person as
Nature, why should we be obliged to defer to her intentions?

We can make sense of this way of thinking only if we put it firmly in a theological setting, in this way. 'Nature' is the pattern laid down by God for men and other creatures to follow. The intentions are not Nature's, but God's; and the reason why it is wrong and sinful to oppose Nature is that this would be to oppose God by spoiling the pattern that He has ordained. But the situation is not yet clear. For certainly not everything we do in opposition to the course of nature can be counted as sinful. Thunderstorms, following the pattern of behaviour divinely appointed for thunderstorms, have a natural tendency to wet us through and damage our buildings by lightning. But nobody has ever thought it sinful to thwart this natural tendency by wearing raincoats and putting up lightning conductors. (Even when thunderstorms were regarded as 'acts of God' it was not thought sinful to take shelter from them.) How do we discriminate between those natural tendencies which express the intentions of God, and those which do not?

The most plausible answer goes something like this. If you examine a complicated piece of machinery, such as a washing-machine or a typewriter, you can understand how it came to be made the way it is only if you know what it is *for*. You can find this out by observing it in use. Once you know that its purpose or function is to make dirty textiles clean, or to reproduce words clearly on paper, you can discover why it has just the parts that it does have, put together in that particular way. From the function of the whole you can derive the function of each part (if a part had no function, the makers would not trouble to include it). Then, given a knowledge of what the machine is meant to do, you can distinguish between a good machine and a bad one, that is, one which does and one which does not perform its function effectively. A washing-machine which gets clothes clean is fulfilling its nature; it is a good one. One that does not is a bad one. Similarly, that part is well constructed which enables the machine to perform its proper function. Now examine a living creature, and you will find a similarly complicated—only much more elaborate—structure in which many parts work together for a common end. Living creatures, including men, may be regarded as constructed for a purpose, and each piece of them as being put there to contribute to this purpose, so that one can ask 'What is a man for?'

(The answer, of course, gives a far wider range of activities than those of any humanly constructed machine.) One can also ask 'What is it for?' of each part of the human organism, and each human capacity. Man, according to this philosophy, was made by God for His own purpose. What this purpose is may be discovered by examining a man in action, seeing what he can do and is conveniently constructed to do. We may assume that each of his parts and capacities was put there for something, and we may discover what it is for by examining what can be most conveniently and efficiently done with it. In this way we may discover a criterion for distinguishing between good men and bad men—the good perform their function, fulfil their nature, more completely than the bad; and also a criterion for telling good bodily organs from bad ones. The eye is obviously for seeing; and a good eye is one which sees distinctly both near and far.

Apply this interpretation to the sexual parts and capacities. What are the sexual organs for? To solve this problem we must find something that cannot be done without them, something moreover which contributes to the general purpose of man as individual or species. The answer is obvious. Sexual organs and capacities are for the procreation of children. This is the only purpose for which one must have them, and it is something vitally necessary for the maintenance of human life on earth. Good sexual activity therefore is that which leads to conception; any use of the sexual organs which does not conduce to procreation is a misuse and therefore bad, being an employment for one purpose of something which was given us for another. So at one stroke all the perversions are ruled out as sinful, as contrary to the purpose for which men were sexually constructed. It is worth noting that the obtaining of sensual pleasure is not counted as a legitimate end for which we may use these organs and capacities. That is not what they are for; we were not put into the world just to enjoy ourselves. 'Private individuals have no other power over the members of their bodies than that which pertains to their natural ends', said Pope Pius XI in the encyclical *Casti Connubii* of 1930.

This is the only interpretation of the idea that perversions are 'unnatural' which is even superficially plausible. But, thoroughly examined, it does not make good sense. It will not produce a coherent and tolerable view of sexual good and evil. For men and women differ from machines in a respect which is essential to the argument. They are not merely capable of carrying out purposes built into their structure by their makers, but also of thinking out and adopting purposes of their own. And they differ from other animals in their capacity to reflect on their purposes and exercise choice among different ones. Men are possessed of reason, and therefore are not, like machines, bound to a predetermined course of action. If we were put into the world for a purpose, we must have been meant to work out for ourselves how to make the best use of the materials and capacities given us; otherwise we should not have been provided with an understanding capable of judging of ultimate ends, instead of one geared to carrying out the instructions of instincts or other built-in motors. Human organs and capacities can be used in an immensely wide variety of ways, a variety certainly not yet fully explored. Whereas a machine *can* only work in one way, can only do effectively what it was constructed to do, men can do an indefinitely large number of different things, and live in an indefinitely large variety of ways. Hence it is not possible with men, as it is with machines, to determine the purpose of man from an examination of his structure and observable capacities. There can be no reason for singling out one of his many styles of living and saying that this represents *the* purpose of man, when he is equally well equipped to live in other styles. His nature leaves him uncommitted. A convincing answer can be given to the question 'What are washing-machines for?' But no convincing answer can be given to the question 'What are men for?' except noncommittal expressions like 'the good life'. Man adapts all his capacities to a variety of purposes.

This is true of his sexual capacities as well as of others. If one inquires as to the purpose of mating in animals, a clear answer can be given. Mating behaviour in them is neatly adapted to the purpose of generation. For the most part, they feel sexual desire only for a limited season, when the species needs to be replenished, and mate only when there is a likelihood of offspring being conceived. But human sexuality is not like this. Humans are affected by sexual desire under all sorts of circumstances when procreation is impossible: it is felt by the immature who cannot yet produce children, by the middle-aged and elderly who can no longer do so, by pregnant women and their husbands, and at all phases of the menstrual cycle. How can one reckon as *the* purpose of an act a result which is achieved on only a small fraction of the occasions on which the act is performed? Even so, as the human death-rate has declined, sexual desire has persistently outrun the need for offspring, so that numerous societies have had to find some way of keeping down the population in order to avoid starvation. An examination of the physical structure and working of the sexual apparatus produces an equally unclear result. The male penis and the male orgasm are both essential to procreation. But the female clitoris and the female orgasm fulfil no generative purpose; they have no discoverable function except to make the sexual act more exciting and agreeable.

Even if human sexual capacity could be said to be for the purpose of generation, the argument that it is therefore sinful to use it for any other purpose is fallacious. There can be no good reason for saying that if a thing was designed for one purpose it is wrong to use it for some other purpose instead or in addition. It is not sinful to use a screwdriver for opening a pot of paint, though that is not what screwdrivers were meant for. It is not sinful to use one's teeth for untying knots, one's breath for cooling one's porridge, or one's intelligence for solving crossword puzzles, though it cannot be maintained that these are the purposes for which these gifts were conferred upon us. It is equally absurd to argue that, because the gift of sexual potency was conferred upon us for the purpose of producing children, it is therefore wicked to use it for some other purpose, such as the giving and receiving of sensual pleasure.

The logical foundations of the theory being unsound, we might expect inconsistencies to arise in trying to apply it. So they do. If we take quite seriously the principle that sexual intercourse is only justifiable when it is 'suited to generation', we are forced to the conclusion that it is wrong to make love to a woman when she is pregnant, when she is past the child-bearing age, or when she is in the 'safe period', if we know when that is. But this is too much even for theologians. So they have allowed that, besides the primary purpose of mating, which is the production of children, there are also secondary purposes, namely 'mutual help, the fostering of reciprocal love, and the abatement of concupiscence'.* But now, may the sexual act be performed for the sake of these secondary purposes alone, when the primary purpose is not fulfilled? If it may not, it must still be wrong to perform the act during the safe period, or when the woman is past child-bearing or pregnant. If it may, if one may use one's sexual powers merely for the fostering of reciprocal love or the abatement of sexual desire, the whole objection to the perversions on the ground of unnaturalness collapses; for a perversion simply consists in the performance of the sexual act in order to obtain relief or to express love under circumstances in which it cannot lead to procreation.

A similar dilemma arises over contraception. In times of heavy infant mortality it was feasible to maintain a position of outright condemnation of all contraceptive devices. In the present age of 'population explosion' this position is plainly untenable; the Churches have had to abandon their traditional ban on contraception, just as in a former age of commercial expansion they had to abandon their traditional ban on lending money at interest. The Protestants have in effect given up the ban. The Catholics, more heavily committed to Aristotelian philosophy, and under the government of a priesthood insulated by celibacy from any intimate understanding of the nature of marriage and the woman's point of view, have held out longer. Their present position (under review) is that the 'safe period' method of contraception is permissible but other methods are not. It is hard to see any morally relevant distinction here, and hard to avoid suspecting that Catholic families are being restricted to a difficult, psychologically trying, and unreliable method of birth-control for no better reason than the reluctance of their leaders to admit openly that they have changed their minds.

There are other inconsistencies. It is, for instance, denied that men have the right to 'frustrate the purposes of nature' in their own bodies; but nobody has questioned their right to do so in the bodies of animals, whom they freely castrate for their own convenience. How comes it that we may use the bodies of other animals as we please to serve our purposes, but not our own bodies? Again, how can one make out that the purposes of nature are frustrated by a man

* Pius XI, *op. cit.*

who, having begotten as many children as his own income or his wife's health can properly cope with, uses contraceptives to avoid further pregnancies, but are not frustrated by another man who remains celibate and produces no children at all?

We conclude that the doctrine of 'natural ends' cannot be coherently stated or consistently applied. If there is anything wrong with perversions, this cannot be shown by calling them 'unnatural', an expression to which no clear and morally relevant meaning can be assigned. We are dealing once more with a set of rationalisations thought up to justify opinions derived from quite different sources. Among these sources we must certainly reckon a puritan hostility to sexual enjoyment. As late as 1945 the British Council of Churches declared: 'The use of contraceptive methods is to be cut out and condemned entirely wherever it is merely an expression of the desire for pleasure without responsibility.' This expresses the misanthropic principle that it is wrong to do something merely for the sake of enjoyment and with no risk of having to suffer for it. It seems to us an immoral principle. Some people professing the same sort of piety argued that it is 'unnatural' and therefore wrong to use drugs to relieve the pains of childbirth, supporting their case by Biblical references to the curse of Eve. But a position defended by unsound arguments may nevertheless be a sound position. It seems improbable that the strong and widespread traditional condemnation of the perversions should be without reasonable justification. Let us take them in turn, and see what harm can be found in them.

Is there anything wrong with masturbation? On this matter there are two things to be said. The first is that, despite widespread persistent beliefs to the contrary, masturbation, even when frequent, is not physically harmful—no more so than normal intercourse. It is not a cause of any disease of body or mind, and people who do it are not in general in worse health than people who do not. Of course, a very excessive practice of this or any other kind of sexual activity can be exhausting and therefore injurious; so can an excessive amount of swimming, reading or eating strawberries. Masturbation can indeed have two kinds of harmful effect. Firstly, a male who has formed the habit of masturbation and kept it up well into maturity may, when he comes to mate with a woman, find himself unable to keep up his erection long enough to give her any satisfaction. In extreme cases, he may find himself ejaculating before he has had time to penetrate her. There is said to be a similar but less serious risk for a girl that she may concentrate all her sexual responsiveness in the clitoris and be unable to transfer it to the vagina, so that she does not experience the deeper kind of orgasm. It is therefore not a good thing to keep up frequent masturbation into adult life if one has any prospect or hope of finding a mate. This argument also holds against 'heavy petting'. The other sort of damage that may be done arises not from the act but from feelings of guilt associated with it. A person who masturbates often and feels ashamed of it may become distracted and anxious to the impairment of his mental health. But this is no justification for the moral condemnation of the practice; quite the contrary, since it is the condemnation which produces the anxiety. The compulsive masturbator is often enough in one way or another an unsatisfied and unsatisfactory personality; it is a habit of those who withdraw from contact with others, and frequent resort to it is a symptom of tension or frustration in other matters. In these cases it can have the same relaxing, tension-releasing effect as intercourse; and this is a point in its favour. Those who in obedience to moral scruples refrain from it may have greater difficulty in achieving tranquillity of mind.

The other thing to be said about masturbation is that most people do it. Nothing is more 'natural' in the sense of being a usual result of the operation of human nature in ordinary circumstances. However often and however severely boys and girls are told that it is wicked, they go on doing it just the same. The effect of the prohibition is not to suppress the practice, but only to increase the risk of setting up tensions in the course of a futile attempt to stop it. For many young people the sexual appetite is in effect irresistible; the attempt to dam it completely cannot succeed. If by the exercise of self-control a boy succeeds in preventing any voluntary sexual activity, he will instead get involuntary sexual activity in the form of nocturnal emissions ('wet dreams'), probably at a rate of something like once a week. Is it worth while expending so much will-power to turn a conscious and somewhat pleasurable emission into an unconscious one?

Much the same sort of thing can be said about the use of the mouth and hands in stimulating a sex partner. Nobody has been able to show that these practices do any harm. Used in sexual foreplay, they often enable a woman to derive pleasure from penetration itself which she would otherwise have missed. They sometimes provide a substitute when for some reason penetration is inadvisable. They are a form of enjoyment without penalty; it seems to be this and this only that the puritan holds against them. Of course, some people find them distasteful; they can do without them.

Now for homosexuality. What is there to be said against a man for whom other men or boys replace women as 'sex objects', or against a woman who prefers other women or girls? Since they get sensuous pleasure from homosexual activity which they cannot get, or cannot get so satisfactorily, in other ways, since nobody is obviously the worse for what they do, what can be wrong with it? If we reject the 'unnaturalness' objection as a baseless rationalisation, where are we to find the source of the hostility which is being rationalised?

We can make use of one important clue. The indignation aroused is almost entirely concerned with *male* homosexuality; lesbianism, though quite common, attracts little attention or concern. While in Great Britain homosexual acts between males are criminal offences carrying severe penalties, similar acts between women are ignored by the law and carry no penalty. Why this discrimination? It is found already in our Old Testament code, which provides the death penalty for male homosexuals, but makes no mention of lesbians. Obviously the discrimination belongs to the double-standard morality, which for once bears more heavily on the male than the female. Perhaps we can understand it better if we bring it into relation with the responsibility of the male to found a family and replenish the stock. The homosexual shirks this responsibility, he spills and wastes the seed that should be making the next generation. If unmarried, he is failing in his duty. If married, he is giving to some other man the sexual gratification and personal affection which he owes his wife. There is a set pattern of family life to be followed, and he fails to follow it and so weakens respect for it. It is of no use for him to protest that his love affairs present examples of as much faithful, generous affection as can be found among heterosexual couples. This makes matters worse. His offence is not just that he has an odd way of amusing himself, but that his affections are misplaced. A man who loves or is loved by another man behaves like a woman, and so upsets the basic division of roles between the sexes. Similarly, in some moral codes, including our ancient Hebrew code and that of St Paul, it is a serious offence for a man to dress like a woman or vice versa (this was one of the charges brought against Joan of Arc, and regarded as weighty). A woman who 'wears the trousers' claims the status of a man, to which she is not entitled.

If one pair of homosexuals is an annoyance, a society of them will be regarded as a menace. For they constitute a dissident group, not merely in their sexual practices but in their rejection of the masculine pattern of life; they threaten the tradition of family life, of male leadership and female subservience. By contrast, what women do with their sex lives is of smaller account. In a patriarchal society, lesbian proclivities will not prevent a woman being married and bearing children perforce; and if she is frigid with her husband, this can even be counted to her for virtue. No group of lesbians threatens the masculine establishment. This, then, seems to be the main source of the abhorrence felt for the 'abominable crime'. Homosexuals may be tolerated where their manliness is not in question, as with the pairs of soldier-lovers found in some ancient Greek communities. The stereotyped popular image of the 'pansy' is of a smooth-faced, mincing fellow with a high-pitched voice and girlish giggle. The image is false; though the girlish type exists, it is rare, and many homosexuals are physically muscular and 'manly'; but the image does show that it is the supposed femininity of homosexuals, their defection from their social role, which is felt as an outrage by masculine men. So we are not surprised to observe that the Criminal Law Amendment Act of 1883, which made British law against homosexuals much more severe, was passed just three years after the Married Women's Property Act, the first great step in the emancipation of women. The fight over male supremacy was on, and the ranks were being closed.

If the fundamental objection to homosexuals is their failure to play their appointed social roles as men or as women, the force of this objection will vary with the degree of differentiation of male and female roles in a community. In industrial society this differentiation is unusually small. Where there is no longer a rigid division between men's and women's work, and it has become common for men to take their share of the housework while their wives take their share of out-of-doors earning, it seems to matter less if one man chooses to act as housekeeper to another man of whom he is fond, or one woman acts as breadwinner while another keeps house for two. It is difficult to object to a homosexual as shirking his masculine role if there is no clearly discernible masculine role for him to play. In fact, many students of the matter believe that in recent generations there has been a large increase in homosexuality in industrial societies. If this is a fact, it may be connected with the decreasing distinction between male and female roles, which weakens both external and internal obstacles to a person's crossing the boundary and taking the role of the other sex.

There is however one field in which the distinction remains clear. In family life, two parents are biologically necessary to produce children, and, it would seem, psychologically desirable to bring them up. The homosexual is usually a person who opts out of family life and parenthood, produces no children, and deprives whoever might have been his wife (or her husband) of the opportunity for family life. A community of such people stands apart from and at odds with the rest of society. A selfish, pleasure-seeking pattern of living is common among them, not because they are constitutionally like this, but because their manner of life leaves them less incentive and opportunity for the taking of responsibility. They rarely achieve the full personal relationship between partners that marriage makes possible. Love affairs are indeed common amongst them, but they are usually short-lived; they lack the support of law and custom, and the common interest in offspring which carry many married couples over awkward periods in their relationship. They lack the satisfactions as well as the responsibilities of parenthood. They can hardly avoid some degree of estrangement from their normal associates; they are uncomfortable with heterosexuals of both their own and the opposite sex.

Two grounds of complaint against them are without much substance. That they do not add to the population, which used to be a reproach, is now, in an age of excessive birth-rates, rather a point in

their favour. And the objection that they are more likely than
heterosexuals to be law-breakers, while there is some evidence in
favour of it, admits of a convincing reply. Homosexuals respect the
law rather less than other men because the law is their declared
enemy; pursued by the authorities on account of their sexual irregu-
larities, they may be expected to hit back at their attackers, and to
suffer greater temptation to other sorts of law-breaking. Their greater
propensity to crime, if it is a fact, is a consequence of the legal and
moral censure to which they are exposed, and provides no justification
for this censure. (There is no evidence that lesbians, who are not
pursued by the police, are less law-abiding than normal women.)
Indeed, some of their criminal acts are the consequences of being
blackmailed; and the blackmailing which leads them into crime would
obviously be impossible if homosexuality were not condemned by
law and custom.

But ignoring these two charges, there is good enough ground in the
rest of the indictment for judging the homosexual manner of life in
either men or women as inferior to the normal, and the homosexual
as something of a misfit in society, at least so long as family life forms
the standard pattern. Granted that this way of life is one to be
avoided if possible, how should our moral codes deal with it?

There is a case for saying that it should not be a matter for moral
judgement at all. For, it is argued, homosexuality is an involuntary
condition; those who are in this condition could not help getting into
it, and cannot now get out of it by any effort of their own. They are
to be pitied, perhaps, but not condemned. Some people suffer from
claustrophobia—they cannot bear to remain for long periods in small
stuffy rooms. This may make them rather a nuisance to those who
live with them, but it would be absurd and unjust to send a man to
prison for being claustrophobic. Homosexuality is like claustrophobia, and it is equally absurd and unjust to punish a man for a
condition which he cannot avoid. It is also unjust to penalise him for
getting the only kind of sexual gratification that is possible for him.
And it seems an unwarrantable interference if the authorities should
try against his will to rid him of his perversion by courses of psychia-
tric treatment which are usually painful and often unsuccessful.
Punishing homosexuals will not make them less homosexually

inclined (if it takes the form of imprisoning them in single-sex prisons, it may have the opposite effect). It is therefore mere wanton cruelty.

Now this argument would be convincing if homosexuality were in every case a condition clearly marked off from the normal, fixed in early childhood, and alterable, if at all, only by very drastic measures. It would not matter whether it was much influenced by hereditary constitution (a point on which experts disagree) or entirely the result of emotional stresses in childhood, so long as the condition in the adult was something which he could not alter. Unfortunately the facts are much more complicated than this. It seems that both normal and perverted tendencies exist in different degrees in all of us. Most people are to some extent and on some occasions susceptible to homosexual as well as heterosexual desire. So besides those who are fixed in a purely homosexual attitude and incapable of feeling any erotic attraction except for members of their own sex, there are others who can be more or less strongly attracted to either men or women, and whose desires are therefore capable of being influenced by social pressure. If a person, especially a young person, has the possibility of developing in either a homosexual or a heterosexual direction, and we are convinced that the latter is preferable, we are justified in trying to ensure that he develops in that direction rather than the other. So, while it would be wrong to punish a homosexual for an emotional condition which he cannot alter, it is not wrong to try to prevent him from infecting other people with his disability. We do not blame a man for being a carrier of typhoid; but we do interfere with his freedom of movement and occupation to prevent his passing the disease on to other people. So we need not blame or punish a person of settled homosexual disposition for having sexual relations with others of the same kind; but we should blame him or her for strengthening homosexual tendencies in other people whose emotional development is still undetermined. The aim of a reasonable moral policy would be not to deprive of physical and emotional satisfaction people who can get it only in the homosexual way, but to prevent the development of this disposition in people whose attitudes are still malleable—this will mean especially young people.

It is easy enough to lay down this general principle, but not easy to say how it should be applied in practice, because we know rather little about the causes of homosexual tendencies. We know that the circumstances most favourable to homosexual *practices* arise when large numbers of people of one sex are living together without the company of the other sex, as in army camps, prisons and boarding schools; so that parents who send their sons to boarding school and magistrates who send young delinquents to Borstal are exposing them to a substantial risk of homosexual temptation. (The fact that most boarding schools are single-sex seems to show that, whatever the law may say, public opinion reckons the risk of homosexuality as a smaller danger than the risk of fornication.) We also know that with most people the homosexual interests arising in circumstances of this kind are superficial and transient: most of the boys who accept homosexual advances at school grow up normal, and plenty of sailors who are homosexual at sea go after the girls as soon as they reach shore. In the same way, very few of the boys who are seduced by adult homosexuals, or seduce them, as sometimes happens, are permanently affected. But in the interests of the few who *are* permanently affected, homosexual seduction of the young seems clearly to be avoided and condemned. In the individual case, a wise morality will probably advise a homosexual to try to change his desires where a change is attainable without great disturbance of the personality; but it is not easy to be sure when this is the case. Some homosexuals are better left as they are; and some have made disastrous marriages in the mistaken hope that marriage would effect a simple cure. The general moral condemnation and ostracism of homosexuals would have some justification if we could be sure that it guides a large number of doubtful cases into heterosexual channels. But whether it really does this is not at all easy to determine.

As to bestiality, lacking any testimony from the dumb creatures chiefly affected, we cannot show that it does much harm. But on the other hand there can hardly be anyone to whom it would be an appreciable loss to be deprived of it.

The case in favour of birth-control is obvious and strong. In the first place, man being a rational animal whose good lies in the subjection of impulse to reason, it is a gain that his procreative powers should be brought under rational control. It is a gain that men should be able to plan the increase of their own numbers, as they already plan the numbers of their domestic animals, with regard to general human benefit, and not just have to endure this increase as a visitation from blind natural forces. Contraception provides us with a method of controlling our numbers that is far superior to the barbarous methods of castration, abortion and infanticide to which men resort in the absence of effective contraceptives. It is a gain that parenthood should be a privilege desired and voluntarily accepted, instead of a penalty imposed on people in the course of fulfilling an instinctive urge. It is a great gain that unwanted children should not be born; for they stand a relatively poor chance of being either happy or good. It is probably worse to be born unwanted than to be born poor, deformed, fatherless or in slavery. It is hard to see a good defence for a policy which aims at multiplying the numbers of the world's unwanted children.

In the second place, world population is now too large for unrestricted breeding to be beneficial. If married people mate as frequently as they feel inclined, without contraception, large families will be common, and will become commoner wherever the standard of nutrition improves. Large families have advantages and disadvantages: advantages in the liveliness of incident and in the social training they give their members; disadvantages in the heavy calls they make on the care and attention of the parents, especially the mothers, and of course, unless there is abundant outside help, on their financial resources. When more babies died in infancy than survived, as has been usual throughout most of human history, large families were necessary to maintain, let alone increase, the population. In these circumstances large families were a public benefit. But now that most babies survive, there are many parts of the world in which large families are a public danger. The human race cannot adequately feed its present numbers. In such countries as India every achievement in increasing production for the improvement of the standard of living is cancelled out by the growth of population, so that instead of there being as many people as before, but with adequate nourishment, energy and the resources for a satisfying life, there are a larger number of people still underfed and near-destitute. Restriction of breeding is an essential step towards lifting the world's poorer peoples out of their dire poverty. Certainly the food supply could be much increased; but not fast enough to catch up with the increase of population if breeding remains unrestricted. The wealthier countries are not at present faced with this problem, because they have been practising birth-control for some generations; but they can escape it only by still more birth-control. And the pressure is not merely on food and water; it is on living space, on the opportunity for privacy and for escaping the nervous strain which in man as in some other animals seems to result from continual immersion in large crowds. An unrestricted birth-rate threatens in the end to spread over the face of the earth that unease, nervous instability and propensity to disorder which now characterise large cities. Thus, quite apart from the advantages to individuals of small families (and the structure of modern industry presupposes working mothers with small families), there is a paramount public need for a restriction on the number of babies.

Five methods are possible: infanticide, abstinence, abortion, sterilisation and contraception. Infanticide can be ruled out. It has been a common method in the past among both savage and civilised peoples; the ancient Greeks killed a large proportion of their female infants as a matter of course. But we are no longer sufficiently callous to adopt it. Abstinence can also be ruled out as a general solution. It requires an exercise of self-control which few people are ready to undertake, and if attempted by married couples it is likely to lead to emotional stress between them; even St Paul advises against it.

Abortion is another matter. In Japan and some Eastern European countries, where abortion is not illegal, it has become the principal means of birth-control, and has produced spectacular falls in the birth-rate. Hungary, for instance, reduced its birth-rate from 21 per 1,000 in 1950 to 14·2 per 1,000 in 1960, in which year there were nearly 16,000 more abortions than live births.* In Japan, abortion seems to have been more important than contraception as a check on population.

In the Western moral tradition, however, it is generally condemned. Some Christian moralists class abortion with murder and refuse to

---

* Data from K. H. Mehlan in *Proceedings of the Third Conference of the International Planned Parenthood Federation*, Warsaw, 1962.

countenance it under any circumstances, on the ground that an embryo is already a human being. But this view is not now generally accepted. An embryo of a few months' growth is not yet recognisably human, and there is nothing to show that it possesses a human soul. Abortion destroys a potential human life, not an actual one. Nevertheless there is something morally repulsive about first begetting a child and then destroying it, and most countries in the Christian tradition treat abortion as wrong and forbid it by law. Making abortion criminal no doubt reduces the number of abortions, but they remain very common. There are of course no reliable figures for illegal abortions, but in Great Britain they are roughly estimated at around 100,000 a year, while in France, where contraceptives are hard to obtain because of legal restrictions, there are believed to be as many abortions as births. Some of the women seeking abortions are unmarried, and fear the alternatives of either bearing and bringing up an illegitimate child or marrying an unsuitable husband, but the majority are married women who already have children; their fear is that another pregnancy and childbirth, another child to see through the long period of dependence, will make all the difference between satisfactory family life and a régime of shortages and discomforts with a permanently tired and fretful mother.

Clearly, legal prohibition does not prevent abortions. But it does make them far more dangerous, for they have then to be performed by unauthorised back-street practitioners who are prepared to break the law, and who are often unskilful and careless. A properly performed abortion is not dangerous, especially if it is done in the early months of pregnancy. In general, it is a good deal less dangerous than childbirth, or such routine operations as the removal of the appendix. Some psychiatrists have laid much stress on the psychological damage resulting to a woman from voluntarily ending her own pregnancy, but it is hard to see how they can be entitled to claim that this is greater than the damage that would have resulted from her bearing an unwanted child. But illegal abortions are dangerous. Their after-effects have been estimated to kill 10,000 Frenchwomen in a year; and besides the risk of injury to the mothers, there is also the risk that an unsuccessful attempt at abortion may cause the child to be born defective. It is clear that very many women will get their abortions illegally if they cannot get them legally, and that so long as abortion remains a criminal act many of them will suffer in health and some will die.

Abortion may be generally condemned, but condoned under exceptional circumstances. There is a case for terminating a pregnancy when the child is likely to be born defective, when the mother is extremely young or has been the victim of rape, or when her health will be in danger if the pregnancy is allowed to continue. The last is allowed as an exception by some legal systems which condemn abortion in general. But 'danger to health' is a vague condition to interpret, especially when one takes into account danger to mental health, which cannot be ignored but is very difficult to assess. In practice, when it is left to the doctors to decide whether there is enough danger to health to justify an abortion, different doctors will decide differently, and whether a woman gets an abortion or not will depend on whether she can find a sufficiently compliant physician or psychiatrist, or pay a high enough fee for his consent. It seems in any case somewhat presumptuous for anybody other than the mother-to-be to decide whether her reasons for refusing to bear and rear a child are adequate. Her unwillingness is itself a powerful reason, since if a child is unwanted to this degree its chances of happiness will be much diminished.

Since abortion does involve the destruction of a living thing at least potentially human, and since it involves some risk of physical or mental injury to the pregnant woman, it seems plainly a worse alternative to contraception as a means of checking the growth of population. But this is so only if contraceptive devices are reliable, cheap, easily available and carefully employed. These conditions are not easily satisfied. Abortion is often the last resort of people who have used ineffective contraceptives, or used effective ones carelessly, as well as of people who cannot get hold of them or afford them. There are even some who prefer abortion, when it can be easily and safely obtained, to the systematic use of contraceptives, which involves trouble at the time and may be a hindrance to spontaneity; this attitude appears to be common in Japan, though less common than it was. And of course there will always be undesired pregnancies resulting from the impulsive actions of people who neglect precautions they could have taken had they been in a more prudent mood. Efficient contraception would not completely dispose of the problem of abortion; but it does seem strongly preferable as a general method of limiting the birth-rate.

Sterilisation, like abortion, is a drastic means of birth-control, a last resort for those who cannot effectively use contraceptives, with the disadvantage that once performed it may prove to be irrevocable. Thus the case for contraception seems extremely strong.

Two sorts of people nevertheless oppose it. Some of them are extreme nationalists, who think that the members of their own nation (whatever it may be) are superior to those of other nations, and therefore the best possible world would be the one with the largest number of their compatriots in it. Or they are expecting an armed conflict with other nations and suppose, mistakenly, that modern wars can be won by weight of numbers.

Contraception is also opposed by some religious groups, both Christian and non-Christian. If, in this as in other cases, the talk about 'unnaturalness' conceals more solid objections, what really lies behind the religious opposition? Partly, perhaps, as with the nationalists, the fear of being outnumbered by unbelievers. Partly mere conservatism, always strong in religious communities, so that a Church persists in an attitude which was reasonable enough in the period of heavy infant mortality in which its views were first formed, but is less reasonable in present circumstances. Partly it is the puritan morality, which is offended at the idea of people enjoying sexual pleasure without having to pay for it. But largely it is fear of the effect of widespread contraception on general sex morality. The religious objectors are afraid that if contraceptives are put openly on sale and prescribed by doctors, they will be used not only by married people to limit the numbers of their children, but also by both married and unmarried to conduct illicit liaisons free of the risk of begetting illegitimate children. This risk being one of the strongest checks on fornication and adultery, they look upon the availability of contraceptives as a main cause of unchastity, and they fear that when they become accessible without restriction sexual morality may collapse altogether. From this point of view, the merit of the 'safe period' technique is that it can be effectively employed only by married couples living together who can choose their occasions for mating—it is no use for casual or furtive liaisons.

There is justification for these fears. Contraceptives have certainly played a part in the loosening of sexual morals over the last couple of generations. Perhaps it has not been a decisive part; contraceptive methods of some sort have always been known and used by those who had need of them, and many present-day young libertines do not use them even when available. Still, those who wish to preserve pre-marital chastity and marital fidelity, and would like to keep the risk of pregnancy as a threat to the unchaste, have this reason for objecting to contraception. But, if one grants the need for enforcing these rules of chastity, one may still question whether it is justifiable to deny the use of contraceptives to married couples on the ground that they may be misused by the unmarried or the adulterous.

6

Attitudes and Problems of Today

In English-speaking countries, people who are over 50 have witnessed major changes in moral attitudes to sex. These changes accompany and probably spring from changes in the pattern of economic and social life. Before they got under way, Western society was firmly based on the family, with Father at its head. Children were dependent on their parents for support, education and opportunities in life, and wives on their husbands for everything. So both wife and children were subject to the authority of the head of the household; to quote a popular saying now almost forgotten: 'When Father says Turn, we all turn.' The sexual morality of that type of society therefore functioned to maintain the cohesion of the family group and the authority of the father. Divorce, if permitted at all, was difficult and uncommon. Daughters were strictly supervised to ensure their chastity on the wedding day. All rules of chastity were applied more laxly to men than to women.

Today, this system has been considerably modified. Children are less dependent on their parents, for the state now provides most education and plays an increasing part in physical welfare. When youngsters leave school few of them work in the family farm or business; they usually find jobs and sources of income outside the family circle, which makes them increasingly independent of it. At the same time women have become able to earn in far greater numbers and at far higher rates than formerly, invading the professions and commerce; thus they are freed from economic dependence on their own menfolk. Moreover girls, being educated similarly to boys, are no longer inevitably inferior to them in knowledge of the world and ability to make themselves a place in it. Mothers too, even the older ones, watch television programmes of topical interest along with the rest of the family, and it can no longer be assumed that they know nothing of what is going on. So Father's claims to superior know-ledge have melted away and his authority has crumbled.

The effects of all this on sex morality can be seen in two ways. First, divorce has become easier and commoner. When, apart from domestic service, nursing, the stage, and being a governess, the only possible career for a woman was association with some man, the break-up of her marriage was a disaster for her and her children. She and they needed the strict laws and customs relating to divorce for their own protection against flighty husbands. But to a woman who can earn her own living and get public assistance towards maintaining her children the prospect of divorce is no longer so catastrophic, financially at any rate. Public opinion no longer con-demns divorce but rather insists that unhappy marriages ought not to be prolonged. So little by little the conditions for obtaining divorce have become easier. Then secondly, the emancipated woman striving for equality of opportunity with men in careers and politics also demands equal rights in sexual matters—the ending of the old double-standard morality. She claims an equal right to choose her marriage partner; more and more openly, girl hunts boy. Inside and outside marriage, she expects sexual gratification, her ration of passion. During our own lifetime there have appeared manuals of sexual technique designed to tell respectable women how to go about getting it. Marie Stopes in 1918 with her *Married Love* set going a revolution in women's attitudes to their sexual rights; the book ran through seven editions in 14 months and we personally have heard how it changed the outlook of women in our parents' generation. In educated circles, and today perhaps more generally, the man who takes his gratification without seeing to it that his partner gets hers is regarded with indignation. Marie Stopes wrote for people who wanted to obtain sexual satisfaction within married life, but other women have gone further and looked for it, as men do, in extra-marital relationships both before and during marriage. So it is no longer possible for men to work the system of sexual morality for their own convenience alone. The new economic independence of young people has brought about similar results for them too. No longer in bondage to their parents, they see the rules of premarital chastity as unnecessary hindrances to natural freedom, and in great numbers reject them as they reject other features of their parents' nominal code of morality.

Kinsey's survey of American sexual behaviour in the 1940s* revealed that 71 per cent of men and 20 per cent of women admitted to premarital intercourse in their teens. Schofield,† dealing with English teenagers in the early 1960s, found 34 per cent of 18-year-old boys and 17 per cent of 18-year-old girls‡ already fully sexually experienced. No figures comparable to those of the Kinsey and Schofield surveys exist to prove that there has been an increase in teenage unchastity, but we cannot believe that the rate was so high when we were young. It emerges from Schofield's detailed results that favourable opportunities, such as being left in the house alone, play an important part in the premarital intercourse of teenagers; when we were unmarried it was not customary for courting couples to be left with the house to themselves, and the unsupervised teenage party was simply not heard of.

So contemporary moral attitudes to extra-marital sexual experience in the industrially advanced countries have become far more tolerant. We might put it that the modern tendency is to reject patriarchal and puritan principles in favour of romantic self-fulfilment. Sexual activity is regarded as fully justified whenever it yields rewarding experiences to the couple, whether or not it contributes anything to the maintenance of the family as an institution. It can therefore be accounted a good thing between an unmarried pair and a bad thing between marriage partners to whom it brings no joy. On this view, a marriage lacking in emotional satisfactions really ought to be dissolved. For romanticism makes the personal happiness of mating individuals the overriding consideration in its sex morality, to which marital fidelity must take second place.

* A. C. Kinsey and others, *Sexual Behaviour in the Human Male*, 1948; *Sexual Behaviour in the Human Female*, 1953.
† Michael Schofield, *The Sexual Behaviour of Young People*, 1965.
‡ This probably is an underestimate, since the married were excluded from the sample, 15 per cent refused interview throughout six attempts, and divergent results from different interviewers suggest that some girls had not been candid.

How far is it desirable to take this romantic view in the present-day world? Here the experience of the Soviet Union is illuminating. Communist theorists took a radically romantic attitude towards sex morality (as we understand the term 'romantic') and drew just those conclusions that we have been mentioning—equality of sexual rights for men and women, easy divorce, and tolerance towards extra-marital sexual relations. In Marxist theory all human institutions have an economic origin. The patriarchal family is founded on male monopoly of earning power and accumulated property, and leads directly to the subjugation of women and the subordination of all personal feelings to economic interest. Marxists argued that, given the alteration of the economic system so that private ownership and inheritance of large-scale property is abolished and women become wage-earners on the same level as men, a different kind of family life will inevitably develop in which man and woman are equal partners and their sex life is determined by affection or passion alone. In 1884 Engels wrote: 'The modern individual family is founded on the open or concealed domestic slavery of the wife. The first condition for her liberation is to bring the whole female sex into public industry, and this in turn demands the abolition of the monogamous family as the economic unit of society. . . . Full freedom of marriage can only be established when the abolition of capitalist production and of the property relations created by it have removed all the accompanying economic considerations which still exert such a powerful influence on the choice of a marriage partner. From then on *there is no other motive except mutual inclination.*' He concluded that in an enlightened society there would be no obstacles to divorce. 'If only the marriage based on love is moral, then only the marriage in which love continues. . . . If an affection definitely comes to an end, or is supplanted by a new passionate love, separation is a benefit for both parties as well as for society—only people will then be spared having to wade through the useless mire of a divorce case.' And in 1914 Lenin declared: 'One cannot be a democrat and a socialist without immediately demanding complete freedom of divorce, for the absence of this freedom is the super-persecution of the oppressed sex—woman.'

In the first period of their rule the Soviet authorities completely accepted this point of view. Divorce was made immediately and automatically available on request to either partner in a marriage. At the same time the rights and duties of 'common-law' spouses living together without a formal ceremony were made much the same as those of married couples. And the rights and duties of illegitimate children towards their parents were made precisely the same as those of legitimate children—in fact, the distinction was abolished. In addition, abortion was made legal. The state declared itself officially indifferent to the sexual fidelity of its citizens.

This position has since been abandoned. In 1936 abortion was once more made illegal unless danger to the life or health of the woman could be proved, on the ground that living conditions in the Soviet Union had become so delightful that no reasonable woman could want to have an abortion.* In 1944 a new code was enacted in which the distinctions between legal and 'common-law' marriage, and between legitimate and illegitimate children, were restored. Only registered marriages now give rise to any rights and duties between husband and wife; only legitimate children are entitled to claim support from their fathers. Divorce by slot machine was abandoned too. According to the present law, divorce can only be granted by order of the court after a formal procedure which is, by design, both slow and expensive. Cause has to be shown and the court must try to bring about a reconciliation. Anyone who sticks it out to the bitter end normally gets his divorce, but at the cost of much time, money and trouble. The state has reasserted its concern in the sexual morals of its citizens; love is no longer a purely private matter. The 1944 code represents an about-turn on the part of the Soviet rulers. The family, once denounced as a means to female slavery and a source of reactionary sentiments, is now upgraded into an essential part of the socialist community, a school of morality, loyalty and love.

Why this about-turn? It represents a return to realism. Although Lenin had seen freedom to divorce as a safeguard against the persecution of women, in practice it is the women who suffer most from a system of slot-machine divorce. The divorced man can easily find another mate, but the deserted woman with children is gravely handicapped in her attempts to get herself another husband. Their father may indeed be made financially responsible for them, but a

* Abortion was once more legalised in 1955.

weekly allowance cannot compensate those deserted for the absence of husband and father. The unwelcome truth is that a woman who wants to be free to change partners should avoid having children. For what children need is a stable family background, with the same father year in year out. New fathers are not only new and alarming faces to the very young; often they have unaccustomed ideas of discipline, unaccustomed ways of living. So, as long as children continue to be reared by their own parents, the community has an interest in the dignity and stability of marriage as the framework within which both mothers and children can find security. Only when the state itself takes over the rearing of children can it afford to disregard the quality and duration of sexual partnerships. Of course the ultimate objective of communist theory is the replacement of the family by the state. Instead of a collection of independent rival families, there is to be a single great brother- and sisterhood to which everyone will be loyal. Children will be raised in institutions, where they cannot be harmed by the follies of their parents. The Russian leaders may still entertain this as a long-term aim; their extensive development of nursery schools and their current expansion of boarding-school education could be interpreted as moves in this direction.

A social system of this kind was described by Plato in the *Republic* more than 2,300 years ago. He suggested that, among the ruling class, the family should be abolished, leaving men and women economically free and equal partners in the enterprise of administration. Matings, strictly temporary in character, would be arranged by the inner ring of rulers on eugenic grounds without regard to the inclinations of individuals; the resulting offspring would be reared in state crèches, not knowing who their actual parents were but regarding with respect and affection the entire group of possible parents. Any children of illicit sexual unions would be put outside the city to die. For this arrangement Plato advances these reasons: that family obligations divert the energies and interests of men and women from their duties to the community, and that few parents understand how best to rear and educate their children. His scheme also has the great advantage of freeing intellectually able women from bondage to domestic tasks so that they may serve the state and develop their own minds. In these days of advanced education for women and shortage of domestic labour, Plato's scheme looks tempting. The same theme has been further developed, drawing on scientific techniques still to be invented, in Aldous Huxley's *Brave New World*. Huxley suggests that the authorities of the future might neuter the eugenically less desirable part of the community and leave them free to amuse themselves sexually at will. From the women who were allowed to become pregnant the fertilised ova would be excised, split to form many individual foetuses to be reared in bottles in laboratories, moved out into the air at the right time, and brought up in batches subject to various kinds of conditioning. Contraceptives would be carried and used as a matter of course by all fertile women outside their scheduled breeding times. With such complete control over conception, it is not surprising to read that organised communal sex orgies would be a standard form of entertainment. This scheme combines the advantages of sexual freedom for all and the production of a population tailored and trained to the needs of society as a whole. Sexual *morality* vanishes entirely from the picture. Once the state has gained control over the production and training of children, no reason remains for it to interfere with other sexual activities. Only a system of this kind, in which breeding is regulated and the responsibility for raising children is the state's and not the parents', can offer complete sexual freedom and complete equality between men and women. Such systems also have the great merit of providing the maximum scope for improvement of the human stock. Yet despite the freedom and equality between the sexes which has long been the romantics' goal, Huxley's system yields nothing like the self-realisation that they expect—on the contrary it gives occasion for little but the sensual self-indulgence of brief and trivial contacts.

Most people on first reading these proposals feel alarmed and affronted; their disregard of human nature seems too flagrant. What could be the drawbacks of a social system of this type?

Let us begin with the children. Every study of the psychological development of children so far has pointed towards the conclusion that their best chance of mental health and happiness is to grow up in the care of their parents or of people who take the place of parents, loving them with a special affection and giving them a feeling of belonging to the sheltering family group. Without this, a child grows up lacking in the capacity of love, or even to take a friendly interest in other people. Further, the boy requires a father and the girl a mother to use as a model for his or her personal development. Only close attachment to a small stable group of people can enable children to grow into responsible, well-balanced adults, capable of being happy oftener than unhappy, ready to co-operate with their work-mates and neighbours and to marry and bring up children of their own. Large institutions do not provide effective substitutes for the natural family; the institution child is said to be only too often affectionless. There seems indeed to be something in human nature that demands a family to grow up in. (Perhaps this is also true of other related animal species.) So to abandon the family would be to take an enormous risk of psychologically maiming the human race.

A second objection lies in the value of the marriage relationship to the married couple themselves. Of all human relationships the most deeply satisfying and rewarding is that between husband and wife, first as lovers, then as partners preparing a home and rearing their children in it. In spite of their quarrels and other limitations, the ordinary marriage that works provides them with something they cannot find elsewhere, positive reassurance amid doubts and disappointments. Nobody save the couple themselves has the full opportunity of perceiving what their relationship means to them; even as their children we cannot know it all. This sort of marital relationship is less easily achieved in a society where there are wide differences between the interests, pursuits, powers and standing of the sexes. Nor will it often be found in polygamous households, since its nature tends to exclusion of third and fourth parties. It will not easily be achieved where marriages are arranged without consultation of those to be married, especially if the society includes a great variety of personality types and individual interests. Nor is it likely to be common in communities where marriage ties are weak and easily broken, where there is nothing but personal inclination to keep couples together. For the full marriage relationship is an intimate and perpetually developing growth which flourishes on enterprises shared and difficulties jointly faced. Mutual attraction alone is not enough to keep it growing; some other common activity must be found in addition to the cultivation of the love relationship. Indeed, love is itself often a generator of jealousy, possessiveness and struggles for supremacy, so that unrelieved concentration on it can bring about great unhappiness. That is why so many Grand Passions peter out.* For most people the shared enterprise that keeps the marriage going is the rearing of a family. Childless couples will obviously have to look for something else they can do jointly that really matters to them. Without this, and without respect for each other's individualities, married life falls short of what it might be. Yet men and women need marriage, and need it at its best.

In the third place, for many men and most women it is home and family that provide the main centre of loyalty, the chief stimulus to responsibility. Young delinquents often turn into good enough citizens once they are married and have children of their own. Intelligent Borstal boys made it clear to us that most of them looked forward to marriage to put an end to their careers of rebellion against society; only so long as they were on their own in life was there nothing to restrain them from going to extremes. Also, the individual who can live for an ideal or a political movement is comparatively rare; even Plato's proposals for community of wives and children were meant only for a small aristocracy. A social group without family attachments normally tends to be 'bohemian' in character, including many aimless and irresponsible people who may be lively and amusing, but are also unreliable and ill-suited for citizenship in a highly planned community. And the bigger the community, the greater the need of any individual for personal attachments to anchor him, some few people to whom he is abidingly important for his own sake.

Suppose then that on these grounds we think family life worth preserving, and frame our sexual morality with that purpose in view, what rules shall we need?

To begin with, we shall have to retain the outlawing of incest, without which no society has been able to promote family life. The case against incest, as we put it in Chapter 1, applies not only to close blood relations, but to adoptive relations, and in general to all members of the inner family group; but it need not apply to cousins, who in our society are only occasional companions. The incest prohibition involves us in preventing brothers and sisters, parents and

* Tolstoy's *Anna Karenina* illustrates this.

children from sleeping together or becoming over-familiar with one another's bodies. Rules of this kind inevitably inculcate some sense of shame and uneasiness from the start, so that complete sexual spontaneity is impossible in human society.

Next we need rules to make the marriage tie firm and normally permanent. If most marriages are to be lasting in fact, then all must be lasting in intention. Easy divorce can tempt people to take on marriage lightly in the belief that a poor bargain can be set aside. Sooner or later many marriages come under some sort of strain, which they are not likely to survive without patience, generosity and prolonged struggle for mutual understanding. The temptation then is to withdraw from a relationship that may be good in part, because it does not wholly achieve an ideal which may be unrealistic for the couple in question. Instead of this, people should be encouraged to work harder at making their marriages viable.

The strongest protection for the permanence of marriage is given by the traditional Christian sex morality, prevalent throughout Western society until quite recently, in which marriage is treated either as absolutely indissoluble (the Catholic position) or as dissoluble only on the ground of adultery. Of course the law cannot force people to live together who would rather separate; but it can refuse the right of lawful remarriage, and (up to a point) compel a husband to maintain his wife and children whether or not he is living with them. The Christian conception of marriage is that of a contract between two persons to unite their bodies and their lives, 'forsaking all other', for the prime purpose of begetting and rearing children. Love between the spouses may be desirable but is not essential, for the relationship is one of obligation rather than enjoyment. The 'love' that is promised in the wedding ceremony is not a romantic love of self-fulfilment, but a practical love of service and cherishing. This promise can be fulfilled by anyone who tries hard enough; but who could guarantee to be thrilled for the rest of his life by one person and one only? The single justification for ending a marriage conceived in the traditional Christian fashion is breach of the fundamental commitment in the contract, the commitment to physical union and fidelity. Thus impotence is a ground for nullity, and adultery the only possible ground for divorce.

This strict rule has ceased to be acceptable to modern communities. Of the romantic creed this much at least is generally accepted, that it is an essential aim of marriage to establish and maintain a relationship of affection between husband and wife, and that a marriage in which affection is lacking is a failure and might better be ended. Nevertheless the existence of dependent children is a strong reason for couples to stay together even though they are dissatisfied with each other, for children need continuous relationships with both their parents. Yet a home in which there is hostility between the parents (no matter how they strive to conceal it) may well be a worse environment than a home with only one parent or with a substitute for the other. The conflict the parents are trying to hide is commonly sensed by their children as something vaguely menacing that undermines their feeling of security. Better perhaps a clean break? Another risk of the bad marriage persisted in is that it may make its offspring cynical about the value of marriage as an institution. There is no single universal rule as to how the interests of children can best be served.

The traditional view also exaggerates the importance of the physical element in marriage. Harmony in bed is the cement that binds most marriages together while the partners are building up a close community of interests and activities. Yet some marriages, like dry walling, can last a lifetime without cement. A marriage can be worth going on with in spite of sexual infidelities or even outright sexual incompatibility. Sometimes an adulterous relationship provides the necessary sexual satisfactions, enabling a marriage centred on its children or on a non-sexual companionship to continue to the benefit of all concerned. The legal principle that a single act of adultery justifies divorce overstresses the physical relationship. Persistent indifference, unkindness or laziness usually cause far more misery. Adultery has to be taken seriously when it is a symptom of general dissatisfaction with the marriage, or part of a settled policy of indifference or cruelty. Adultery that is merely casual need be no serious threat to marriage. If it were, on Kinsey's findings 50 per cent of American marriages would be wrecked by the husband's adultery, a good deal of which is known to and tolerated by the wives, especially in the working classes. The really dangerous adultery is that involving emotional attachment. Most wives would sooner think of their husbands as inevitably prone to lustful escapades than as emotionally captivated by some other woman.

Thus, eventually, in Christian countries grounds for divorce other than adultery have come to be admitted by the state if not by the churches. In England these grounds are desertion, cruelty and insanity. But the position has remained that marriage is a contract for life which must continue until it is broken by one of these matrimonial offences. There has to be a guilty party and an innocent one, one who breaks the marriage vows and wrongs the other, and one who is wronged and so can claim release from his/her own vows on that ground. The guilty one must suffer for the misdeed in reputation and in pocket; the guilty husband must pay alimony to his divorced wife without having any claim on her; the guilty wife loses her right to be supported by her husband. If both are guilty, then neither is entitled to redress and divorce may be refused.

But if we go this far, ought we not in reason to go further? Is not the plainest case presented for divorce when both parties are agreed that their marriage is unsuccessful and ought to be ended, and should not divorce be granted in all such cases? Cannot a marriage fail without gross misconduct by either partner and be dissolved without convicting somebody of an offence? The traditionalist answer to this plea is that once the principle of divorce by consent is admitted people will be encouraged to separate for frivolous reasons and to marry equally carelessly on the understanding that whenever they want a divorce they can get it. In England this argument has so far prevailed, and the law not only refuses to admit petitions for divorce by consent, it regards 'collusion' between the partners as a ground for refusing a decree. The law does not, however, succeed in its purpose. Divorce by consent does take place, but only between those who are willing to conceal their collusion from the court—sometimes indeed evidence of adultery is successfully faked by partners who wish to be divorced. It would be less hypocritical, and probably no less effective, to admit the principle of divorce by consent, with the proviso that the court can refuse to grant a decree or defer it for a period if they are convinced that the grounds for seeking it are trivial, and that the couple have made no serious effort at marital co-operation.

There does not seem to be a really strong case for hindering the separation of childless young couples who find themselves ill-matched, but might do better with other partners. The number of such cases is bound to increase as more and more inexperienced teenagers are getting married. It is arguable that if we took more trouble to ensure that young people all met a wide choice of partners, and to explain to them how marriage functions, what are its problems, and how to find a likely fit, ill-assorted marriages would become fewer.

Again, why should it not be customary for middle-aged couples who have wearied of each other to divorce and re-marry once their responsibility for dependent children is over? Thus stale and hopeless lives might be revived, especially for women, who tend in middle life to feel that little remains for them to live for, or that they have been cheated. The frigid would have a new chance of joyous union with a new mate. Both sexes would be given motives for resisting the downward slither into a premature old age; the necessary adjustments would prolong their period of flexibility. The darker side of this picture is the forlorn wife or husband deserted in the 50s and no longer capable of attracting another partner. It may be said that without divorce such people are only hanging on to the appearance of a married life. True, but then to some people appearances are what matter most.

There remains the awkward problem of those marriages which have definitely broken down, the parties separated and one of them perhaps living with someone else, but one partner is guiltless of any matrimonial offence and at the same time unwilling to consent to divorce and give the other partner freedom to re-marry. On the one hand, if the rejected spouse is allowed to preserve the empty legal status of marriage, he/she does the unfaithful partner harm without benefit to him/herself (apart from vengeance). On the other hand, to empower courts to divorce 'innocent' parties against their will would remove a major deterrent to those tempted to break up existing tolerable marriages.

Concerning unhappy marriages it may be said that prevention is better than cure. If it is right to dissolve miserable marriages, it is also right to try to prevent them from ever being contracted. To limit sex education in schools to bald accounts of the physiology of reproduction is short-sighted; young people are eager for further information, not only about methods of contraception, but about the emotional and psychological aspects of sexual relationships at various levels. Boys would like to know more about what makes girls behave as they do, and vice versa. There are dozens of popular delusions to be scotched among the inexperienced; more important, so far as is possible, fascinating mysteries should be replaced by factual knowledge as a basis for married life. An adequate grasp of contraceptive techniques might lessen the numbers of shotgun weddings, which carry the worst risks of breakdown. Perhaps we ought to make it more difficult for people to marry at all, treating marriage as the reward for apprenticeship well served. Like literacy it is easily available to all, and like literacy too often undervalued.

We turn now to the form of sexual behaviour that arouses most discussion at the present day—premarital intercourse. Few people are now shocked by divorce; many still are by premarital sex, especially when it takes place among the young.

Sexual intercourse outside marriage is also common in certain groups of older people who either do not wish to marry or are unfit for marriage by ordinary standards. There are those whose mental or physical condition would render them undesirable mates or parents but who do not consider themselves thereby precluded from all sexual contacts; there are the abnormally restless, irritable or introverted, the vagabonds of all ages, the mainly homosexual or lesbian, and many whose occupations or preoccupations tend to prevent stable married life, such as sailors, explorers, entertainers and spies, people always on the move and never on hand when most needed by a family. The same applies for reasons of emotional rather than physical remoteness to those who are obsessed by some Cause. For all of these a morality prohibiting sexual gratification outside marriage seems unnecessarily harsh. And they may well be less troublesome to the community as lone wolves than as defaulting spouses. If these people are going to have children, they ought to be properly married and try to abide by the rules of marriage. But provided that they take care not to beget children why should the community insist on their marrying? It is not as though we still needed children from everyone to keep up our numbers; on the contrary, in most countries we are rapidly moving into a situation in which many people will have to be discouraged from having children if living conditions are not to become too cramped.

But with the majority of young people the case is quite different. They intend in the long run to marry and raise families. Can we reasonably require them to remain chaste until they do?

There are four lines of argument in favour of premarital intercourse: that it relieves boys, and even some girls, of the prolonged strain of continence until they can afford to wed; that boys should be sexually skilled before they marry; that marriage should never be undertaken for reasons of physical attraction alone, and therefore these should be deprived of urgency by premarital experiment; and that any sexual incompatibility should be discovered before marriage through a long apprenticeship with the intended partner.

Firstly, it is said that it is very harsh to make young people wait for sexual experience until they can afford to marry, which in the case of boys undergoing professional training or apprenticeship may well be nine or more years after puberty. The situation is aggravated because a boy's sexual desires are at their most urgent and his potency at its peak during the middle and late teens. It follows that to insist on celibacy is to impose long years of tension and strain, which can only be eased by masturbation or homosexuality, neither of them in boys a good preparation for happy married life. Moreover, this period of strain due to enforced sexual continence is being steadily extended in both directions, puberty commencing earlier and earlier, and the educational process being protracted later and later into adult life.

Against this argument there really seems nothing to be said. It is indeed the most important of the four, as has long been recognised. Only lip service, and not always that, has ever been paid to the principle that boys should remain chaste until they marry. Had girls been in general as ardent as boys, it is doubtful whether the sexual double standard would have been so widely accepted by both sexes as it has been in many civilisations. In fact, most girls are able to wait for marriage without undue discomfort, so that this argument concerns them mainly as the fiancées or steadies of lively boys. Should they yield to the boy friend, or leave him to find sexual outlets elsewhere? According to Schofield, most girls do not want sex before they marry, and about a third of the whole sample, including twice as many girls as boys, actually supported the old premarital double standard. Male support for the double standard emerges more plainly in the avowed wish of half the boys to have premarital sex, whereas only ten per cent said they were willing to dispense with virginity in their wives. Kinsey found a similar situation, startlingly accompanied by the claims of many lower-class boys to have had intercourse with hundreds of different girls. The troublesome question here is: with whom do the boys get or expect to get their experience, if not with girls they may ultimately marry? Teenagers do not expect to pay professionals for their sexual pleasures. Nor is it likely that many of them go to bed with married women. Schofield argues that there must exist a small group of highly promiscuous girls who satisfy large numbers of boys whom they pick up or are casually acquainted with, and this view is supported by the proportions of experienced boys who said that their partners were pickups (42 per cent) or 'short affairs' (26 per cent). Over half of them had had intercourse with more than one partner. It is doubtful whether this promiscuity in a substantial minority of boys differs much from one era to another.

Secondly, it is urged that satisfactory love-making requires skill, chiefly in the man. In a marriage between virgins the wife is likely to wait a long time before her husband learns how to satisfy her sexually. Has she not a right to expect him to know his job as a sexual initiator, just as he has a right to expect her to know how to cook and keep house for him? This argument also has some force. Girls suffer from the bungling and impatience of their husbands; some, looking back, would prefer to have had them broken in by other women, and perhaps even equipped with testimonials!

A third argument is that neither boys nor girls should be constrained to marry merely in order to satisfy their sexual urges or their curiosity, for neither curiosity nor appetite alone can form a sufficient basis for lifelong marriage. 'Better leap into bed every time and work it out of your system,' runs this argument, 'and then when you do eventually decide to marry it will not be for sex alone but with someone whose companionship you cannot do without, someone who will share your interests and values, a lifelong friend and partner in the rearing of your children.' On this view marriages based on physical attraction alone are risky businesses, only too likely to turn out unhappy and to form a poor environment for children. The only good sort of marriage has everything.

Linked with this is the fourth argument which asserts that, seeing how sexual incompatibility can ruin a match, every couple should 'taste and try before they buy'. Some pairs are incapable of adjusting to each other and it is better to discover this before the wedding. Of course, this implies that premarital intercourse between engaged couples would take place regularly, in bed, without feelings of guilt or apprehension, and over a period of many months. Only if a sexual fit can be found should marriage be undertaken. Patience and regular practice make up the recipe. We should go into training for married life as we would for an athletic contest! Since no snatched love affair would count as serious training, this is clearly not an argument in favour of promiscuity. It represents the extreme reaction against the practice of the groom's deflowering his bride on the wedding night without adequate preliminary physical courtship, one which no doubt has caused countless brides to react against sexual intimacy and remain frigid to the end of their married lives.

These two arguments in favour of premarital experience for *both* sexes are less convincing. To take first the argument that a good marriage will not be based on mere physical attraction and that therefore people should hurry into bed with those who appeal to them sexually to discover whether the attraction is going to last, whether if lasting it is more than physical, and whether if merely physical it is enough to compensate for any clash of temperament or values. The mistake here is to suppose that a good marriage can be founded on nothing but sexual attraction. Although it is impossible to find out what proportion of marriages are so founded, one may guess that sexual attraction plays a key part in very many. When we fall in love we cannot usually give a coherent account of why it is with this particular person and not with someone else whose tastes more nearly resemble our own; we are actuated by a blind drive towards This One, the more helpless because we cannot point to any clinching reason other than that it just is so. The behaviour of the beloved may puzzle us, his/her views may exasperate us, but no matter, this is the one preordained by fate to enslave us. But where is the evidence that such marriages are notably less satisfactory than those between people who coolly choose each other on account of matching tastes and values? Mutual sexual attraction enables couples to construct a working relationship which lasts until their children are grown up; what more is needed? The romantic search through many beds for the relationship which has everything can outlast youth, leaving behind it a wake of disillusioned partners and in the seeker the dreary conviction that it was unrealistic to be so exacting. Nor is the experience of being lovers necessarily a reliable guide to what the partners may expect as man and wife. The two relationships are far more different than the unmarried would suppose. Simply by committing oneself in wedlock, one sets in motion an unending series of small adjustments which cumulatively bring about the marital accord. Sensible spouses do not try to alter each other, but through the years they unknowingly become more alike in habits and outlook so that it has been observed of some pairs that they even *look* alike. We who are writing these words seem to have developed a written style in common, but if we had not married, if we had simply taken a trial trip, it is doubtful whether we should have envisaged the gradual dissolving away of our marked differences of habits and opinions. Our point is that until two people commit themselves by marrying, there is not enough incentive for them to overcome their differences. They are unable to tell beforehand whether a companionable fit will be possible or not. At the opposite extreme are those who believe themselves well-matched when they are not and never will be, and are unlikely to find this out so long as they are not actually sharing a home.

The same counter-argument applies to the view that it is better to detect physical incompatibility in the course of a premarital love affair than to find it out after the wedding. Obvious physical repulsion shows itself at an early stage of courtship: halitosis, sweaty feet, lack of personal fastidiousness, sexual over-avidity, all reveal themselves as soon as the couple begin to explore each other. But the actual physical adjustment of postures and techniques leading to simultaneous climax may take years to achieve, admittedly coming more readily when neither has formed the habit of self-tension against any sexual response. Once again, it is the couple committed in marriage who have the most incentive and the most opportunity to make a success of their physical partnership however long the apprenticeship may have to be. Since a substantial proportion of married women* fail to experience climax during the first year of married life, how long would a trial run have to continue before it was deemed a failure? If lovers relied on achieving full sexual satisfaction before agreeing to marry, great numbers would never marry at all. There is indeed something to be said for marrying the one you know can respond to you, but given time and patience so might many others; ease of sexual response is not enough as a guide in selecting a spouse —the quick responder may not for long attract you. And as long as premarital intercourse is not generally approved of, there is the additional difficulty that it cannot be undertaken by most young people regularly in bed and free from anxiety, furtiveness, haste or guilt. But unless these conditions are satisfied the experience is not of much value as a test.

If premarital intercourse cannot be relied on to sort out either the physically incompatible or those who are capable of achieving a companionable fit, it cannot be recommended as a device for improving marital selection. A longish courtship with sex play stopping short of intercourse is likely to prove at least as effective. So the only telling arguments in favour of premarital intercourse favour it for boys but not girls, leaving us with the old sexual double standard. This position is confirmed by the arguments *against* premarital intercourse, most of them of more concern to the girls.

Of these the most important is the risk of pregnancy. In 1964, 63,000 illegitimate children were born to English women (1 in 14 of all births) and another 75,000 had babies within eight months of their wedding days. Anyone who stops to think about this must be struck by the unnecessary stress and unhappiness involved in many of these pregnancies. In addition there were an unknown number of abortions, all of them causing emotional stress and many of them danger to health. When girl marries boy because she is pregnant, even if marriage has always been considered possible between them, it may come prematurely from the financial point of view, when they have nothing saved and the boy is not yet earning enough to keep

---

* In Kinsey's sample the proportions vary with educational level from 34 to 22 per cent.

three. But if marriage was not intended at all, one or both partners may feel they have been trapped. Where no marriage takes place and no abortion, the unmarried mother, unless her family help her, must either let the baby be adopted or engage in a heroic struggle to support it *and* look after it. The illegitimate child itself lacks its natural father, for whom there is rarely an effective substitute. To be brought up by a widow or divorcee is far from ideal, but to be reared by a woman whose lover has rejected her (or who has rejected him), is likely to prove even more of a handicap. The child is at abnormal risk of being either overvalued or treated as something of a nuisance, impairing his mother's chances of marriage. As he grows older, loyalty to her may distort his attitude to other people and spoil his own hopes of marriage.

This objection to premarital intercourse would lose much of its force if fully effective contraceptives were both available to unmarried people and regularly used by them. At present there seems to be no form of contraception which can be guaranteed both effective and safe, but doubtless there soon will be. But it is clear both from the numbers of illegitimate conceptions and from Schofield's investigations that many young unmarried people who are sexually active are not seriously trying to avoid pregnancy. Only 20 per cent of sexually experienced girls in Schofield's sample always used birth-control methods and as many as 61 per cent said they never did. Assuming that they left the responsibility to the boys, still 55 per cent of the experienced boys did not regularly attempt birth-control. Just half these boys said either that they did not like contraceptives or that they did not care. About 40 per cent of them had no clear idea of what they would do if their girls became pregnant. And among those who had not yet had intercourse fewer than one in four of boys and about one in six of girls cited fear of pregnancy as the deterrent. Apparently the risk of pregnancy is not taken seriously by large numbers of English teenagers. Even if contraceptives were made available by clinics catering for the unmarried, we cannot assume that illegitimate pregnancies would cease to be a serious problem.

A second argument against premarital sex is from the risk of venereal infection. These diseases are contracted and transmitted by people who are more or less promiscuous. This is therefore an argument against promiscuous sex but not against intercourse preliminary to marriage where neither partner is unfaithful. Indeed if this were a regular practice the risk might be lessened. At present in England it is not a very large risk but it is disturbing to find that three-quarters of the boys and four-fifths of the girls at risk in Schofield's sample would not recognise the symptoms if they were infected. One of the obvious gaps in British sexual education is this lack of precise information about venereal disease; such information is imparted in, for instance, West Indian schools.

Another group of arguments which seem to have more effect on young people seek to show that in one way or another premarital intercourse spoils their chances of happy married life. Of course, so long as the masculine preference for virgin brides persists, a girl who has premarital intercourse is at a disadvantage. But leaving this preference aside, is there any reason to suppose that those who have been unchaste before marriage will make less faithful and less satisfactory husbands and wives? The view that unchastity becomes a settled habit which marriage will not alter is plausible, but where is the evidence to support it? Similarly it is often said that premarital unchastity renders young people callous and emotionally unresponsive. This seems to apply not to an honest search for a life partner, but to premarital *promiscuity*, about which it may be said that it is likelier to be a sign of selfish irresponsibility than the cause of it. There is a further and less disputable argument which mainly concerns girls: owing to her organic and psychological differences from a boy, a girl will probably find that after intercourse she is more emotionally involved, at the very point at which the satisfied boy might be losing interest in her. The emotional risks of being jilted are greater for her now than they would have been had she remained virgin.

What clearly emerges from these pros and cons of premarital intercourse is that if we are more permissive about it, most of the advantages will be reaped by the boys. For the girls carry the heavy risks of pregnancy and emotional involvement and at the same time stand a poorer chance of enjoyment, needing prolonged courtship and skilled partners. Much the strongest argument against premarital intercourse is the risk of illegitimate pregnancy. Whereas a couple may be able to make a good case for having intercourse before marriage, they can make none for having it without contraceptive precautions.

But even if *we* are convinced by the arguments against premarital intercourse, it is clear that in their present temper many young people will reject them. (45 per cent of the boys in Schofield's sample and 24 per cent of the girls denied that sexual intercourse before marriage is wrong.) They can be kept chaste only if they are effectively chaperoned as they were by our grandparents and still are, for instance, in Portugal today. If we leave them unsupervised the social pressure of their own age group towards a sexual 'keeping up with the Joneses' may easily push into each other's arms boys and girls who have not especially lively passions and do not really enjoy intercourse. Because sex is 'with it' they resolutely go through the ritual. If adults cared enough about premarital chastity they could check all this by taking care not to provide opportunities such as unsupervised teenage parties and leaving youngsters to keep house while they go on holiday. It is unrealistic and unfair to abuse them for their sexual behaviour without trying to lessen the temptations.

There is of course an important difference between the love-making of 'steadies', who may some day get married, and promiscuous sex relations. If we cannot hope to reverse entirely the trend toward greater freedom of sexual activity among the young we could at least draw a sharper distinction between intercourse intended as a preliminary to marriage, and promiscuous sex. It might be possible to establish some such principle as this: that one should not go to bed with just anyone who is around, casually, out of curiosity, or to allay physical appetite, as one might eat an ice. People should only mate when they are fond of each other and are thinking of marrying. Intercourse would then be taken as a declaration of serious intention. If society is prepared to accept this principle, then it must be unambiguously accepted. Mothers must be ready to make up double beds for their engaged children. Betrothal would become once again a public commitment from which people would only withdraw for grave reasons.

The alternative to this procedure would be to expect the engaged to limit themselves to 'heavy petting', as widely practised in America and to an increasing extent in England. More information should be given about it in the course of sex education so that its drawbacks can be appreciated; for instance, that those who venture so far cannot always be certain of resisting the tug of the whirlpool, and that some women will learn to prefer this type of stimulation to normal intercourse.

Since ultimately it is the young people themselves who have to take the decision as to their sexual conduct, the least we can do for them is to provide them with all the relevant information. We could only safely keep them ignorant if we were willing to chaperone them strictly, and under modern conditions in the English-speaking countries this is out of the question, even though we do limit their opportunities. Schofield found that two-thirds of the boys learned what they knew from their friends and only one in nine received information from their parents. Girls were better treated, but still as many found out how conception takes place from their friends, as from parents and teachers put together. Much of what passed for information was inaccurate. There is a strong case for a thorough, perhaps uniform, programme of sexual education in all schools covering not merely the physiology of reproduction but birth-control, venereal disease and the psychology of sex. This instruction should be given in easy stages, beginning at junior level with the biological side. By the age of 13, most are ready to be confronted with the psychology of the sexes and discussions can begin with no holds barred. Instructors would have to be married, and should have undergone a course of special training so that they would be ready for any question. It is important that they should be able to secure the confidence of their audiences, which inexperienced teachers would not do. Within this framework the strong reasons for premarital chastity in girls would be clearly seen. Some instructors would want to take the line that premarital intercourse is morally wrong. Boys and girls who are incapable of seeing it that way, however, should be trained to ask themselves what course of action is likeliest in the long run to bring about happiness for those concerned. This is the only way to forestall the common tendency to do first and think afterwards, for instance to treat the risk of unwanted pregnancy as negligible. The principle of promoting happiness for those concerned would also exclude trifling with the feelings of others, leading them on to love when we know that reciprocation is unlikely, or inducing desire that we do not intend to satisfy, whatever our reasons may be.

The most blatant form of sexual exploitation is prostitution, a two-way form of exploitation. For the man who mates with a woman for money is using her only as a means to his own gratification without regard for her well-being, and she in turn uses his desire to extort money from him without any sort of kindly feeling or respect for him. So the physical union wherein true lovers should express their mutual delight becomes a market deal between two people who if they feel anything at all for each other may easily feel contempt. But the objection is not only at this level, where it can be equally true of an unsatisfactory marriage. There is the further objection that prostitution can hardly ever be a satisfying way of life for a woman. Financially profitable it may be, but it is also disagreeable and insecure; prostitutes have to be paid both 'danger money' and 'dirty money'. Most sacrifice their chances of being either respected or loved—for they in turn are often exploited by their own boy friends or ponces.

Yet the prostitute can claim that she performs an indispensable function in society (as we have seen that even St Augustine recognises). In an ideal society she would have no place, but as things are she provides a safeguard against the more widespread seduction or rape of chaste women by gratifying the sexual appetites of unattached men. Many attempts have been made to rid a community of prostitutes; they always fail. Just as rationing inevitably produces the black market, so the attempt to limit sexual activity to marriage inevitably produces a supply of illicit sex provided by the prostitute. Why should we not regard her then as performing an unpleasant but necessary service to the community to which no particular disgrace need be attached? This attitude is common enough in some Asiatic countries: in Japan, for instance, a girl can spend a few years earning herself a dowry in a brothel, without damaging her prospects of respectable marriage. Even the European tradition is not quite consistent in this matter: high-class kept women have been able to gain acceptance in some aristocratic circles as they could not have done among the middle classes. The arrangement provides a substitute for polygamy in a monogamous society.

If any odium there be, it should fall rather on the men who create the demand than on the women who supply it, but even they have their excuses. It may be preferable to resort to a prostitute instead of seducing a friend of the family when the wife for any reason is not available. Perhaps as equality between the sexes increases we may find male prostitutes catering for the needs of women.

What is reasonable and necessary is to require that in conducting their business prostitutes shall not be a nuisance through public importuning, through the setting up of rowdy brothels in quiet residential districts or, above all, through the spreading of venereal disease; all these are matters for official regulation.

This raises the question of the proper relation between sexual morality and the law, on which there are sharply opposed attitudes. Some people hold that sex is a private affair with which the law has no concern so long as those involved do not make public nuisances of themselves. Others maintain that it is the business of the law to express and uphold the general moral standards of the community, including its sexual standards, and to punish any actions which are thereby accounted wrong by those standards. On this view, if adultery, homosexuality and fornication are considered wrong, people ought to be punished for committing them.*

The first point of view is difficult to maintain. For one thing, an act cannot be regarded as a purely private matter if it leads to the birth of a child. For another thing, the health of a community does depend on the security and vitality of its family life, and sexual practices which tend to the impoverishment of that life are a social evil. The life of a libertine, homosexual, prostitute, abortionist or pornographer is not lived in a closed cell; it makes a lot of difference to the general atmosphere of living whether such people flourish or not. Sexual customs are implicated in the economic relations between men and women, the arrangements for the upbringing of children, the formation of friendships, alliances and social groups; the sexual rules of a community are among the institutions by which it preserves

---

* For this controversy see P. Devlin, *The Enforcement of Morals*, and H. L. A. Hart, *Law, Liberty and Morality*.

its way of living, its distribution of power and responsibility, its machinery for the transmission of culture to the next generation. If men keep harems or girls have illegitimate children, public policy and the public weal may be involved.

In particular, it is not reasonable to regard it as an entirely private matter how many children a couple choose to have. The sum of these private decisions determines the quantity and quality of a country's population. Whether it has too large or too small a population in relation to its resources, whether that population is increasing rapidly and burdened with crowds of children, or decreasing and burdened with crowds of pensioners, these things make a huge difference to its welfare. A couple are not morally entitled to think only of themselves and their offspring in deciding the size of their family, or whether they will have a family at all; they must also consider the public interest. And it is proper for the authorities to have regard to this interest by offering advantages and disadvantages; by giving family allowances, tax rebates, scholarships, school meals, and so on, to encourage people to have children if a declining population is foreseen; by withdrawing such advantages and making contraceptives and abortions easily obtainable if they expect overcrowding. Again, there is a public interest in encouraging procreation among those whose children may be expected to be intelligent and temperamentally stable, and discouraging or even preventing it among those whose children are likely to be mentally defective, very dull or temperamentally unbalanced. These latter find it increasingly hard to be either useful or happy in mechanised modern society and their care makes high demands on the energies of abler people. One can hardly admit an unlimited right of such parents to produce similar children. If there is no public concern for these matters, there will be a tendency for dull-witted and irresponsible people to have the bigger families, and for the prudent, those who are ambitious for their children, and those women who are able enough to have careers, to produce the smaller families, to the detriment of the general level of ability and character. It must be part of the business of law and morals to encourage such breeding behaviour as will improve the human material of our civilisation. It is not of course possible to predict with certainty whose children will grow up defective in intelligence or personality, but it *is* possible to distinguish couples who are very unlikely to give their children either a heredity or an environment conducive to normal development. Many insane, feeble-minded and criminal individuals are already prevented from breeding by being segregated in institutions.

While it is reasonable that government and public opinion should try to influence sexual behaviour with a view to the common good, it by no means follows that the law should try to enforce *all* the accepted standards of sexual morality. This project runs into two practical difficulties. Firstly, laws about sexual behaviour are very hard to enforce, because most of it takes place in private. Unless an accomplice confesses, adultery, fornication and homosexuality can go undiscovered. (In a high proportion of divorce cases involving adultery, the adultery could not be established without the co-operation of the guilty person.) An unenforceable law is worse than useless. It is unjust in its operation because it is a matter of chance which few individuals get caught and punished; and since it can be broken with impunity, contempt for law in general is encouraged. While it does not prevent the evils at which it is directed, the attempt to enforce it commonly produces evils of its own. The law against homosexuality provides British blackmailers with a good part of their income; and those relating to prostitution subject the police to strong temptation to corruption and perjury.

The second difficulty about enforcing the accepted standard of sexual morality is that on many important points no accepted standard exists. In public affairs one sometimes has to disregard minority opinion and make dissenters toe the line. But this is justifiable only when the advantages of conformity are obvious and the evils of deviation great. The ill effects of sexual non-conformity, apart from illegitimate births, are not obvious; they are matters for speculation. Although we suspect that a community of sexual libertines would be less happy and prosperous than one of sexual puritans, we cannot prove it; still less can we prove that the presence of a few libertines in a generally sedate society does clear and substantial harm. And this would need to be shown before the intervention of the law could be justified. There is a decisive difference here between sexual offences and offences such as fraud and violence.

The problem of the legal regulation of pornography is especially subject to this difficulty. When people earn money by portraying sexual intimacies and stimulating sexual fantasies, one readily comes to suspect that their activities do harm in stimulating desires that would be better left quiet. But this suspicion is hard to confirm by evidence. When the paperback publishers of *Lady Chatterley's Lover* were prosecuted for obscenity, the defence produced plenty of worthy people who swore that they had read the book without being corrupted by it. To make good its case, the prosecution should have produced some unworthy characters to swear that they had read the book and *had* been corrupted by it; no such evidence was given. The influence of sexy novels, paintings, films, songs and photographs can only be guessed at. It seems quite likely that people who are disturbingly stimulated by pornographic elements in what they see or hear would, if censorship were more severe, discover the sexually stimulating in what now seems inoffensive. So much in our environment is potentially sexy. So very much in the products of the fine arts gets some of its appeal from touching more or less lightly this emotional nerve centre. There are elements that could be sexually stimulating in classical statues, the works of Rubens and Titian, Wagner and Cole Porter, Shakespeare and the Bible. A censorship that tried to eliminate this feature altogether would mutilate all the arts, in attempting the impossible task of distinguishing what is from what is not capable of sexually disturbing its audience.

What conclusions have emerged from these discussions of ideas about sexual morality? In the first place, it is clear that we do need a morality of sex—to prevent the violence and disorder of a sexual free-for-all, when every woman would be the prey of any man who could catch her, some men would catch no woman, and no child but the toughest could survive the inevitable neglect while all this was going on. Sexual morality, whatever form it takes, supplies the mechanism of family life, to protect women during their long periods of helplessness in pregnancy and to provide children with the continuous care they need from both parents over many years. If human sexual behaviour were merely seasonal, if pregnancy lasted a few weeks only, and the human infant were as quick to reach independence as a kitten is, there would be no more need for sex morality among us than there is among cats.

All systems of sex morality may be judged by their success in meeting these needs. The strict patriarchal system, with its separate standards of morality for the two sexes, fulfils them very well; otherwise it could not have dominated most of the civilised world for so long a period. But it succeeds at the cost of complete subjection of women to men, denying them all or most of their freedom of sexual choice, impairing their chances of sexual enjoyment, and turning the marital relation into one of master and servant. In Western civilisation we are no longer willing to accept the subjection and deprivation of women entailed by this system of morality. Nor, even if we wished, should we be able to enforce it under contemporary social and economic conditions. We require a system which recognises the equal standing of the sexes, admitting the woman's right to choose her partner, to change him for sufficient reason, and to co-operate with him on level terms. So we make a demand of marriage which our ancestors did not—that it shall be emotionally (some writers use the word 'spiritually') satisfying to both partners. The romantic movement is an expression of this requirement. St Thomas Aquinas thought that sexual intercourse was a good thing only if it was an expression of marital obligation. Modern moralists are apt to require that it shall be an expression of affection, lasting throughout the joint life of the partners. Many people are prepared to rate emotional satisfaction as a more important function of marriage than the provision of economic security or services to the family. So husband and wife today require more from each other than they did under the law of Moses; they expect to be lovers as well as partners. This sort of marital relation, once achieved, is as far superior to patriarchal marriage as friendship between equals is superior to any emotional relation between master and servant. But it is harder to create, and far more easily imperilled. The risk is that we may ask of the marital relation more than it can reasonably be expected to provide in most cases, and may view as a failure any marriage in which the accord and delight of the lovers is not indefinitely maintained. 'Marriage', said Abraham Lincoln, 'is neither Heaven nor Hell, but Purgatory'— that is, an ordeal to be endured as well as a banquet to be savoured.

Our most pressing contemporary problems in sexual morality, namely divorce and premarital intercourse, are the outcome of our greater freedom. We should judge of all sexual problems on these principles: that whatever threatens the loyalty of husband and wife, and so undermines the security of family life, is wrong, as also is whatever deprives children of a proper family to grow up in. So there is a *prima facie* case against adultery, against slot-machine divorce, and against the begetting of illegitimate children before or after marriage; this last is the gravest of all sexual offences. Beyond this point judgement is hazardous, because we are so largely uncertain of the ultimate effects of what we do.

The best place for sexual experience clearly is within a happy marriage, but it would be altogether too dogmatic to conclude that this is the only proper place for it. There are always those to whom, for a variety of reasons, happy marriage is not possible, and those whose opportunities of stable married life are genuinely unimpaired by extra-marital adventure.

If we aim at stable and happy marriages, we should think more positively of promoting the conditions under which they are likely to come about. At present, too little is done towards equipping young people with the sort of information that would help them to make the best of their relationships with one another, before and during marriage. Nor do we encourage in them a sober sense of their responsibilities as married people. All this is a problem of general education.

Since sex has become more a matter of free choice, it has of necessity become more competitive. Partners have first to be won and then to be held faithful by constant effort to please and charm. In patriarchal society, only prostitutes need to use cosmetics, but in our society today respectable wives use lipstick and eye-shadow, and nice young girls are indistinguishable at sight from the professional vendors of sex. Sexual competition is even implied in advertisements for products ranging from shaving creams to patent medicines. Wherever we turn, our attention is drawn to sex, in stories, films, stage shows, popular songs and even the coloured advertisements for Mediterranean holidays, all of them dominantly erotic in character. There is therefore a risk of our coming to believe not only that sexual experience is an important thing (which is obvious) but that for most people it is the supremely important thing, so that nobody can live a satisfactory life that is not centred on it. This is the present-day myth about sex; it is a serious error, even if not so serious as the puritan error that it supplants. We might indeed get on better both with sex and with sexual love if we made less of a to-do about them, and were less anxious about living up to ideal standards of what they should be.

Our generation has another important problem which our ancestors for the most part escaped. Now that it has become possible for the majority of babies to survive to old age we can no longer countenance the haphazard begetting of children. We must be concerned about the future numbers of people on the earth. We must also be concerned about their congenital endowment, for the low death-rate deprives us of the services of natural selection in preventing physical and mental deterioration of human stock. The need to control both our quantity and our quality is bound to become an increasingly important aspect of sexual morality. It is not as yet so recognised; we are still inclined to think of procreation as a matter of purely personal concern. But we cannot afford to persist in this attitude. Parents of the future will have to undertake this social responsibility, and governments of the future the responsibility for influencing their decisions.

Recommended Reading

S. C. Ford and F. A. Beach, *Patterns of Sexual Behaviour* (1952). Survey of the sexual habits of men and beasts.

E. Westermarck, *History of Human Marriage* (5th edn, 1921). Compendium of information on marriage customs throughout human society.

G. P. Murdock, *Social Structure* (1949). Survey of marriage customs, mainly in primitive societies.

A. C. Kinsey and others, *Sexual Behaviour in the Human Male* (1948); *Sexual Behaviour in the Human Female* (1953). Results of a large-scale investigation of sexual activities in modern U.S.A.

M. Schofield, *Sexual Behaviour of Young People* (1965). Results of an investigation of English teenagers.

A. B. Hollingshead, *Elmtown's Youth* (1949). A study of the impact of social class on sexual and other behaviour of young people in a small American town.

D. and V. Mace, *The Soviet Family* (1963). Description of Russian family life from personal observation.

D. Sherwin Bailey, *The Man-Woman Relation in Christian Thought* (1959). Historical and critical survey.

St Thomas Aquinas, *Summa Theologiae*, III, Supp. 41–68. An authoritative medieval exposition of the Christian view of marriage.

Pope Pius XI, Encyclical *Casti Connubii* (1930).

S. Freud, *Introductory Lectures on Psycho-analysis* (1922); *Civilisation and its Discontents* (1930).

M. C. Stopes, *Married Love* (1918). An early and highly influential handbook of erotic techniques for married couples.

B. Russell, *Marriage and Morals* (1929). By a philosopher.

B. B. Lindsey and W. Evans, *The Revolt of Modern Youth* (1925); *Companionate Marriage* (1927).

A. Kardiner, *Sex and Morality* (1954). By a psychologist.

A. Heron (ed.), *Towards a Quaker View of Sex* (1963).

Report of the Wolfenden Committee on Homosexual Offences and Prostitution, Cmnd 247 (1957).

D. J. West, *Homosexuality* (2nd edn, 1960).

G. Westwood, *A Minority* (1960). The results of a small-scale survey of homosexuality.

Report of the Royal Commission on Marriage and Divorce, Cmnd 9678 (1956).

O. R. MacGregor, *Divorce in England* (1957).

N. St John-Stevas, *Life, Death and the Law* (1961).

R. Atkinson, *Sexual Morality* (1965). A criticism of arguments.

P. Devlin, *The Enforcement of Morals* (1959). On the relation between law and morality.

H. L. A. Hart, *Law, Liberty and Morality* (1963). On the same topic.

Illustrative Fiction

J. W. von Goethe, *The Sorrows of the Young Werther*; *The Elective Affinities* (the most recent translation is entitled *Kindred by Choice*). Influential specimens of the early romantic novel.

Jane Austen, *Sense and Sensibility*. Guying the romantic novel.

Doris Lessing, *The Golden Notebooks*. Detailed account of the emotional disappointments of the woman who believes in free love.

Marcel Proust, *Remembrance of Things Past*: Vol. 2, *Swann's Way*— vivid account of an obsessive love affair and ensuing jealousy; Vols. 7 and 8, *Cities of the Plain*—accounts of homosexual loves; Vol. 9, *The Captive*—more about obsessive love and jealousy.

Leo Tolstoy, *Anna Karenina*. The emotional claustrophobia of 'living in sin'.

Aldous Huxley, *Brave New World*. A forecast of the new society that is completely planned and without sentiment.

Index